Worship in
Spirit and Truth

Worship in
Spirit and Truth

John M. Frame

PUBLISHING
P.O. BOX 817 • PHILLIPSBURG • NEW JERSEY 08865-0817

Unless otherwise indicated, Scripture quotations are from the HOLY BIBLE, NEW INTERNATIONAL VERSION. Copyright © 1973, 1978, 1984 International Bible Society. Used by permission of Zondervan Bible Publishers.

Printed in the United States of America

Library of Congress Cataloging-in-Publication Data

Frame, John M., 1939–
        Worship in spirit and truth / John M. Frame.
                p.   cm.
        Includes bibliographical references (p. 155) and index.
        ISBN 0-87552-242-4 (paper)
        1. Public worship—Presbyterian Church. 2. Public worship—
Reformed Church. 3. Reformed Church—Liturgy. 4. Presbyterian
Church—Liturgy. I. Title.
BX9573.F73   1996
264'.051—dc20   96-6115

Contents

91980

To

Dick and Liz,
Jack and Rose Marie,
Doug and Lois,

who showed me the way

Preface

Worship is something incomparably precious to me. When God led me to faith in Christ, he spoke to my heart largely in the context of worship services—especially the hymns: I just couldn't get them out of my head. And through all the ups and downs of my Christian life, it has been worship that, again and again, has turned my wandering heart back to the Lord.

Nevertheless, I would not have suspected ten years ago that I would now be writing a book about worship. I am, and have been for twenty-seven years, a seminary teacher in the fields of apologetics and systematic theology. I have not been a specialist in the area of worship, and I have not been eager to enter into the controversies of the field.

God has, however, through various events, pushed me to consider the biblical principles of worship. Since the beginning of my Christian life, I have been a church organist, pianist, occasional choir director, and occasional worship leader. For some years, I have served as associate pastor of New Life Presbyterian Church in Escondido, California, for whom I was asked to develop an adult Sunday school course on the subject of worship. I have taught the course six or seven times in the last fifteen years.

My involvement with worship, then, has forced me to respond to controversies. In my denomination, the Presbyterian Church in America, various differences of opinion concerning worship have been expressed. Some of them reflect differences that are in the evangelical world as a whole, while others are distinctive to Presbyterianism. In many ways, I would have preferred to be left out of these discussions. I would much rather worship God than argue about principles of worship. But in view of my background and my deep concern for the subject, it was hard for me to decline to participate in the debates; so, I did enter the discussion. Part of my motivation was a concern to preserve for my local congregation and others like it the freedom to worship God in its accustomed style—one that is nontraditional, but, in my judgment, fully scriptural. These discussions have sharpened my thinking in this area and have given me the desire to share some of my thinking with other Christian brothers and sisters through publication.

Presbyterian worship—based on the biblical "regulative principle," which I describe in these pages—was in its early days very restrictive, austere, and "minimalist."[1] It excluded organs, choirs, hymn texts other than the Psalms, symbolism in the worship area, and religious holidays except for the Sabbath. Presbyterians in the "Covenanter" tradition, such as those in the Reformed Presbyterian Church of North America and a few in other denominations, still worship in this way, but they are in that respect a small minority of conservative Presbyterians today.

Nevertheless, the Puritan theology of worship that produced this minimalism is still taught in theologically conservative Presbyterian churches and seminaries as the authentic Presbyterian and Reformed view of worship. This is partly because that theology is reflected in the Westminster Confession of Faith and Catechisms, to which these churches subscribe.[2] But the Westminster standards actually contain very little of the Puritan theology of worship. The Puritan and Scottish divines who wrote the Westminster standards were wise not to include in them all of their ideas on worship. The principles responsible for liturgical minimalism come from Puritan and other Reformed texts that go above and beyond the confessional documents. Yet these extraconfessional texts themselves have considerable informal authority in conservative Presbyterian churches.

The result has been that although few conservative Presbyterian churches actually worship in the Puritan way, the Puritan theology of worship remains the standard of orthodoxy among them. This discrepancy sometimes leads to guilty consciences. I have talked to pastors, for instance, who are unwilling to go back to exclusive use of the Psalms in congregational singing, yet feel awkward about singing hymns. They almost seem to think that they *ought* to worship as the Puritans did, even though they have no intention of doing so. They worry that this wavering amounts to an inconsistency in their commitment to the Reformed faith and to Presbyterian orthodoxy.

I believe that Presbyterians need to do some rethinking in this area. In my view, the Westminster Confession is entirely right in its regulative principle—that true worship is limited to what God commands. But the methods used by the Puritans to discover and apply those commands need a theological overhaul. Much of what they said cannot be justified by Scripture. The result of our rethinking, I hope, will be a somewhat revised paradigm for Presbyterian worship: one thoroughly Reformed in its assumptions, affirming the regulative principle and the statements of the Westminster Confession and Catechisms, but allowing much greater flexibility than the Puritans did in applying God's commands for worship. Such a revised paradigm will relieve the guilty feelings mentioned earlier, not because it allows us to ignore God's commandments, but because it helps us to understand more accurately what our Lord expects of us.

This book will expound this revised paradigm somewhat, over against the traditional alternative, but I will not be able here to do justice to the historical debate. I hope one day to write another book, longer and more technical, that will enter the historical controversy in some detail. This present book has a more modest purpose: to state simply the main biblical principles governing the public worship of God's people. It is a revised version of the adult Sunday school lessons on the subject that I have taught at New Life, and I hope that other churches will find it useful for such classes. I shall here be writing for adult laypeople and will seek to define clearly any technical terms that come up.

I have included questions for discussion at the end of each chapter. I think the best way to use this book in study classes is not for the teacher to summarize the chapter each week, but for the class members to read the material at home and then meet together to discuss the questions. The answers to the questions will summarize the content of the chapters and will suggest additional areas to explore.

Most of the existing literature on worship is of three types. The first type is historically oriented, advocating that present-day churches make a greater use of the resources of Christian tradition. The second type is ideological, merely reiterating the traditional concepts and arguments of one of the traditional positions: Catholic, charismatic, Presbyterian, etc. The third is more practical than theological, suggesting ways of making worship more interesting, more emotionally satisfying, more intelligible, or somehow more "authentic" as an encounter with God. These three types do sometimes overlap, but most of the literature seems to have one or more of these purposes in mind.

Although I find value in those types of books and articles, this volume will have a different focus. Unlike the first type of literature, this book will focus on Scripture itself. I hold the historic Christian view that Scripture is the very word of God, inerrant and bearing ultimate authority. While I don't deny the value of Christian tradition, I don't believe that such tradition is divinely authoritative. If we are to make legitimate use of tradition, we must first ask what Scripture says. Scripture must define, limit, and warrant our use of tradition. I intend in this book, therefore, to discuss principles that are of greater importance than anything derived from tradition alone.

Nor will this book, like the second type of worship literature, merely repeat a traditional theological position. My own theological commitment is Presbyterian; I subscribe enthusiastically to the Westminster Confession of Faith and Catechisms, and I trust that that commitment will be quite evident in this book. The main assumptions of this book are distinctively Reformed: God is sovereign; he is related to us as the covenant Lord; he wants us to worship only as his word requires.

Some readers may feel that the book is too concerned with issues that have arisen mainly within Presbyterianism. Nevertheless, it will also have an ecumenical thrust. I hope to state the fundamental Reformed principles in a way that will be intelligible and persuasive to Christians from all traditions, and I hope to justify, on the basis of these principles, some forms of worship that are not typical of the Reformed tradition. I will make the case for Presbyterian worship from Scripture, not from church history and tradition. Unlike some Presbyterian writers, I believe that I understand, and understand sympathetically, why some sincere Christians prefer not to worship in the Presbyterian way. I recognize that there are real problems in the traditional Presbyterian view that need to be addressed from the Scriptures, and I intend to deal with those problems seriously. And I believe that there are some things about worship that Presbyterians can learn from non-Presbyterians.

It will not be my chief goal in this volume to suggest techniques for making worship more "meaningful," although I will offer such suggestions from time to time. This book is about biblical principles. It focuses on the question, What does God command for worship, and what does he forbid? It is important to know the answer to this question before we seek human means for improving the worship experience. The first key to meaningful worship is to do as God commands. Beyond that, of course, there is the question of how best to carry out those commands in our own time and place. This is the question of the "language" in which we should express our worship to God and in which we should seek to edify one another. But we must know what limits God has placed upon us before we can determine the areas in which we are free to seek more meaningful forms. One of my main concerns in this book is to define both the areas in which we are bound by God's norms and the areas in which we are set free (by those same norms!) to develop creative *applications* of those norms.

You may be surprised at the extent to which this book, for all its preoccupation with divine norms, focuses on *freedom* in worship. In my view, once we understand what Scripture actually commands for worship, we will see that it actually leaves quite a number of things to our discretion and therefore allows considerable flexibility. I believe that most books on worship, Presbyterian and otherwise, underestimate the amount of freedom that Scripture permits in worship. Historically oriented books typically try to make us feel guilty if we do not follow traditional patterns. Theological traditionalists also typically want to minimize freedom and flexibility. Even those who offer suggestions for "meaningful worship" are often very restrictive, for they tend to be very negative toward churches that don't follow their suggestions.

This book, however, will stress that Scripture leaves many questions open—questions that different churches in different situations can legitimately answer differently. That should not surprise us very much: following God's commands is always the way of freedom. When we substitute human ideas (whether past traditions or contemporary notions) for God's word, the result is bondage to human wisdom. God's yoke, though binding, is much easier and lighter.

I wish to express my thanks to all of those who have prodded me toward this project and stimulated my thinking on these matters. My former pastor, Dick Kaufmann, first recruited me to teach this subject in our congregation. He suggested many ideas to me that have turned out to be seminal in my own thinking, and he gave me much encouragement. In a way, this volume seeks to summarize the thinking underlying the worship of the "New Life" Presbyterian churches: New Life Presbyterian Church in Escondido, California, where I worship, our "mother church" of the same name in Glenside, Pennsylvania, and others. The people mentioned on the dedication page have been associated with these bodies and have made important contributions to my thinking, although they should not be held responsible or accountable for the ideas in this book.

I also wish to thank the Mission to North America of the

Presbyterian Church in America for appointing me to its Worship Task Force. Many of the thoughts of this volume first found expression in papers written for that task force and were the outcome of stimulating discussions with the other members. As in nearly all my published books, I offer thanks to Vern Poythress and Jim Jordan, who, on this topic as well as many others, have greatly influenced my thinking. Thanks also to my critics, especially Edmund P. Clowney, Joseph Pipa, and T. David Gordon, men for whom I have enormous respect, even though on this subject I cannot go in the direction that they would prefer. Their gracious and thoughtful rebuttals have been constantly in my mind as I have written these pages. I am also grateful to Presbyterian and Reformed Publishing Company for their encouragement in this project and to James Scott for his excellent editorial work.

My hope is that God will use this material (and subsequent discussion of it) to edify his people and to motivate all of us to a greater faithfulness in the worship of our triune Lord.

Notes

[1]To quote James Jordan, *Liturgical Nestorianism* (Niceville, Fla.: Transfiguration Press, 1994), 13–19.

[2]The Westminster Assembly, which produced the Confession and Catechisms, also produced a "Directory for the Public Worship of God." But that directory has not been given constitutional status in most present-day Presbyterian churches.

1

Some Basic Principles

What Is Worship?

Worship is *the work of acknowledging the greatness of our covenant Lord.*

In Scripture, there are two groups of Hebrew and Greek terms that are translated "worship." The first group refers to "labor" or "service."[1] In the context of worship, these terms refer primarily to the service of God carried out by the priests in the tabernacle and the temple during the Old Testament period. The second group of terms means literally "bowing" or "bending the knee," hence "paying homage, honoring the worth of someone else."[2] The English term *worship,* from *worth,* has the same connotation.

From the first group of terms, we may conclude that worship is *active.* It is something we *do,* a *verb* (as well as a noun), to borrow from the title of a recent book by Robert Webber.[3] Even at this early point in our study, we can see that worship is far different from entertainment. In worship we are not to be passive, but to participate.

From the second group of terms, we learn that worship is honoring someone superior to ourselves. It is therefore not pleasing ourselves, but pleasing someone else. Immediately the question How can worship be made better? has a focus: better not primarily for ourselves, but better for the one we seek to honor. It may be that worship that is better for him will also be better for us. But our first concern must be to please him; any benefits for us will be secondary.

So, worship is performing service to honor somebody other than ourselves. It is both "adoration and action," to quote from the title of another recent book.[4]

Scripture uses all of these terms on the human level, referring to relationships among human beings. We serve one another, and we honor one another. But there is a special sense in which God alone is worthy of worship. The first of the Ten Commandments says, "You shall have no other gods before me" (Ex. 20:3). God, who is called Yahweh ("LORD") in the Decalogue, is entitled to a unique honor, one that is not to be shared with anybody else. The fifth commandment, "Honor your father and your mother," makes it plain that human beings also deserve honor. But that honor may not compete with the honor we owe to the Lord himself.

The Ten Commandments are the written constitution of a *covenant* relationship between God and Israel. That covenant is a relationship between a great king (the Lord) and a people he takes to be his own. As the Lord of the covenant, God declares Israel to be his own people and himself to be their God.[5] As their God, he speaks to them with supreme authority and thereby governs every aspect of their lives. Their chief responsibility is to honor him above all others. There is to be no competition for Israel's loyalty and affection: "Hear, O Israel: The LORD our God, the LORD is one. Love the LORD your God with all your heart and with all your soul and with all your strength" (Deut. 6:4–5).

Jesus reinforces this teaching: "No one can serve two masters" (Matt. 6:24). It is not only that we are forbidden to worship Baal or Jupiter; we also must not worship money! God claims lordship over every area of our lives. As the apostle Paul says,

"Whether you eat or drink or whatever you do, do it all for the glory of God" (1 Cor. 10:31).

One of the most amazing things about Jesus is that he demands for himself the same kind of exclusive covenant loyalty that the Lord God demanded from Israel. Jesus upholds the fifth commandment against the Pharisees and scribes, who dedicated to God what should have been used to support their parents (Matt. 15:1–9). But Jesus also teaches that loyalty to him transcends loyalty to parents (Matt. 10:34–39). Who is Jesus to demand such service and homage? Only loyalty to God transcends loyalty to parents in God's covenant order, and so Jesus in Matthew 10:34–39 is making a clear claim to be God. Like Yahweh in the Old Testament, Jesus presents himself as the covenant Lord, the one to whom we owe our utmost allegiance (see Matt. 7:21–29; John 14:6).

In worship, we do familiar things—things we often do with one another. Praise, for example, is, or should be, a part of everyday life. Parents praise their children for significant accomplishments and good character. Employers praise their employees, and vice versa, which makes for good morale in the workplace. And God calls us to praise him in worship. But that praise is on quite a different level. To praise God—indeed, to praise Jesus!—is to recognize him as unconditionally superior to ourselves in every respect, as one whose true greatness is beyond our poor power of expression. He is the ultimate object of praise.

In worship, we also express affection, joy, and sadness. We confess our faults; make requests; give thanks; listen to commands, promises, and exhortations; present gifts; receive cleansing (baptism); and eat and drink (the Lord's Supper). These are things we do all the time in our normal relationships with other people. But when we do them in worship, there is something special: we do them for the Lord, the ultimate one, the Creator and ruler of the heavens and the earth; and we do them in Jesus, our Savior from sin. In worship, these common actions become unique, mysterious, and life-transforming because of the one whom we worship. These actions become the priestly service by which we acknowledge the greatness of our covenant Lord.

God-Centered Worship

As we have seen, worship is *homage, adoration*. It is not primarily for ourselves, but for the one we seek to honor. We worship for his pleasure foremost and find our greatest pleasure in pleasing him. Worship must therefore always be God-centered and Christ-centered. It must be focused on the covenant Lord.

In an earlier book,[6] I analyzed three aspects of covenant lordship: control, authority, and presence. The Lord is the one who controls the entire course of nature and history, who speaks with ultimate, absolute authority, and who takes a people to be his own, to be with them. These three aspects of divine lordship are prominent in biblical worship.

In worship, we adore God's covenantal *control*, his sovereign rule over creation. The praises of God's people in Scripture are typically praises of his "mighty acts" in creation, providence, and redemption (see, for example, Ex. 15:1–18; Ps. 104; Zeph. 3:17; Rev. 15:3–4).

To worship God is also to bow before his absolute, ultimate *authority*. We adore not only his power, but also his holy word. Psalm 19 praises God first for revealing himself in his mighty acts of creation and providence (vv. 1–6) and then for the perfection of his law (vv. 7–11). When we enter his presence, overwhelmed by his majesty and power, how can we ignore what he is saying to us? So, in worship we hear the reading and exposition of the Scriptures (see Acts 15:21; 1 Tim. 4:13; Col. 4:16; 1 Thess. 5:27; Acts 20:7; 2 Tim. 4:2). God wants us to be doers of that word, not hearers only (Rom. 2:13; James 1:22–25; 4:11).

And, in worship, we experience God's *presence*. As the covenant Lord, he comes to us in worship to be with us. The tabernacle and the temple in the Old Testament were places where God himself met with his people (Ex. 20:24). The worshiper shouts with joy that God is in the midst of his people (Zeph. 3:17). The name of Jesus, the name in which we worship, is Immanuel, which means "God with us" (Isa. 7:14; Matt. 1:23). In New Testament worship, the presence of God may impress even a visiting unbeliever, so that "he will fall down and worship

God, exclaiming, 'God is really among you!' " (1 Cor. 14:25).

Therefore, true worship is saturated with reminders of God's covenant lordship. We worship to honor his mighty acts, to hear his authoritative word, and to fellowship with him personally as the one who has made us his people. When we are distracted from our covenant Lord and preoccupied with our own comforts and pleasures, something has gone seriously wrong with our worship. As my former pastor, Dick Kaufmann, says, when we leave worship, we should first ask, not What did I get out of it? but How did I do in my work of honoring the Lord?

Gospel-Centered Worship

Adam and Eve enjoyed a wonderful friendship with God. God had created them in his image, and he had declared that they were "good" (Gen. 1:31). Eden was a kind of temple, in which Adam and Eve regularly rejoiced in God's mighty works of creation, heard and obeyed the word of the Lord, and delighted in his nearness to them. But they disobeyed God's word (Gen. 2:16–17; 3:1–6) and defiled their worship. He cursed them and cast them out of their temple (Gen. 3:14–24).

Yet God did not abandon them. Even amidst the curses, God gave to Adam and Eve the promise of a deliverer who would destroy Satan (Gen. 3:15). God continued to speak to them and to seek fellowship with them. He sought worshipers (John 4:23). In Genesis 4:3–4, both Cain and Abel bring offerings to the Lord. In the time of Seth, people "began to call on the name of the LORD" (Gen. 4:26). Worship continued after the Fall.

God blessed worship after the Fall, but he wanted his people to worship him with a consciousness of their sin and guilt, and of what he had done to free them from that guilt and power of sin. Prominent in Old Testament worship were animal sacrifices, which prefigured the death of Christ, "the Lamb of God, who takes away the sin of the world" (John 1:29). As we have seen, God's people praise him, not only for his mighty acts in creation, but for redemption as well. In Exodus 15, the Israelites praise God for delivering them out of their slavery in Egypt. That de-

liverance foreshadowed God's greater deliverance of his people
in Christ from that death which is the wages of sin: "Worthy is
the Lamb, who was slain" (Rev. 5:12).

As in Eden, God's people hear his word in worship. But now
it is somewhat different, for God's word now tells us of our sin
and God's provision for our forgiveness. Again, we fellowship
with God by eating and drinking with him, but that eating and
drinking sets forth the Lord's death until he comes (1 Cor. 11:26).
Everything we do in worship, therefore, now speaks of sin and
forgiveness, of Jesus' atonement and resurrection for us. Worship
following the fall of Adam should not only be God-centered, but
also Christ-centered and gospel-centered. In all our worship,
the good news that Jesus has died for our sins and risen glori-
ously from the dead should be central.

Trinitarian Worship

Scripture presents a history of redemption, a narrative of what
God has done to save his people from sin. As that history pro-
gresses, Scripture presents gradually clearer teaching about the
Trinitarian nature of God: that he is one God in three persons,
Father, Son, and Holy Spirit. We learn of the Trinity, not just as
an interesting fact about God, but because it profoundly concerns our salvation. At God's appointed time, the second person
of the Trinity became a man—Jesus—to live a perfect human life
and to die as a sacrifice for sin. Then, after Jesus' resurrection
and ascension to heaven, the Father and the Son sent the Holy
Spirit, the third person of the Trinity, to empower the church in
its mission to bring the gospel to all the earth. The Spirit applies
the work of Christ to our hearts, he enables us to understand and
apply the word of God, and he fills us with divine gifts, empow-
ering our ministry and testifying of Christ.

When Jesus told the woman of Samaria that "a time is coming and has now come when the true worshipers will worship the
Father in spirit and truth" (John 4:23), he was not merely pre-
dicting a more sincere or heartfelt worship among his people.
Rather, he was referring to the new things that God was prepar-

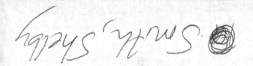

ing to do for our salvation. The "truth" is the truth of the gospel, the good news of salvation in Jesus (compare John 1:17; 14:6). The "spirit" is the "Spirit of truth" (John 14:17; 15:26; 16:13), who comes to bear powerful witness to that gospel.[7]

Worship "in Spirit and truth," then, is Trinitarian worship—worship that is aware of the distinctive work of the Father, the Son, and the Spirit for our salvation. It is Christ-centered: when we "call on the name of the Lord," we call on the name of Christ (Matt. 18:20; John 14:13; 16:24; Rom. 10:9; 1 Cor. 12:3; Phil. 2:9; Col. 3:17). Christ is the Lord in his control, authority, and presence. He is the power of God (1 Cor. 1:24), the authority of God (Matt. 28:18–20), the presence of God tabernacling in the midst of his people (John 1:14; Matt. 18:20; 28:19–20; Rom. 15:9). He is the sacrifice that fulfills all the sacrifices of Old Testament worship (Mark 10:45; John 1:29; 1 Cor. 5:7; Heb. 9:26; 10:12). He is the high priest who intercedes in prayer for his people (Heb. 4:15–16).

Such worship is also worship in and by the Spirit. By the Spirit, we come to "glory in Christ Jesus, and . . . put no confidence in the flesh" (Phil. 3:3). The Spirit is the Spirit of Christ (Rom. 8:9). He does not speak on his own initiative, but speaks only what he hears from Jesus (John 16:12–15). He persuades us that we are children of God (Rom. 8:16), and that the gospel is God's truth (1 Thess. 1:5). As Jesus intercedes for us, the Spirit utters to God the unspoken groanings of our hearts (Rom. 8:26–27).

God-centered worship, following the richness of the New Testament revelation, is always worship in the name of Christ and by the Holy Spirit. The only name by which we may be saved is that of Christ (Acts 4:12), and we can come to know him only by the sovereign working of the Holy Spirit (John 3:3; Rom. 8:14–15; 1 Cor. 2:12). God-centered worship is Trinitarian worship. Our worship should be clearly directed to God as Father, Son, and Holy Spirit.

Vertical and Horizontal

Evidently, then, Christian worship is "vertical," directed to our triune God for his pleasure. The focus of our effort in worship should be on pleasing him. From this principle, some might conclude that we should not pay any attention to human needs in worship. Talk like that can sound very pious, but it is unbiblical. The God of the Bible is not like the false god Moloch, who demanded human sacrifices from his worshipers. Rather, our triune God wants to bless his people when they meet with him. There is no opposition between worshiping God and loving people. Loving God involves loving our neighbors as ourselves (Matt. 22:37–40; Mark 7:9–13; 1 John 4:20–21).

In worship, we should not be so preoccupied with God that we ignore one another. For example, worshipers should not ignore the needs of the poor (Isa. 1:10–17; compare 1 Cor. 11:17–34; James 2:1–7). And we should make sure that our worship is edifying to believers (1 Cor. 14:26). First Corinthians 14 emphasizes the importance of conducting worship, not in unintelligible "tongues," but in language understandable to all. Even an unbeliever, when he enters the assembly, should be able to understand what is taking place, so that he will fall down and worship, exclaiming, "God is really among you" (v. 25). So, worship has a horizontal dimension as well as a vertical focus. It is to be God-centered, but it is also to be both edifying and evangelistic. Worship that is unedifying or unevangelistic may not properly claim to be God-centered.

How can we maintain a horizontal focus that is properly biblical without creating man-centered worship? We should remember that a proper concern for worshipers does not mean catering to their wants. Worship is not, therefore, a program to provide entertainment, or to enhance self-esteem, or to encourage self-righteousness. The best way for us to love one another in worship is to share the joy of true worship without compromise—a joy focused on the good news of salvation. God-centeredness and edification, therefore, are not opposed, but reinforce one another. Worship is a time to care for one another, to build up the unity of our fellowship in Christ (Heb. 10:24–25). We love because God in Christ first loved us (1 John 4:19).

Broad and Narrow

The biblical terms for worship apply to various stated occasions of public worship, particularly the worship at the tabernacle and the temple during the Old Testament period. But they also have a broader meaning, characterizing the believer's life in all its aspects. In Romans 12:1, the Greek term *latreia* (which elsewhere designates the service of priests in the temple) describes the believer's offering of his own body in service to God: "Therefore, I urge you, brothers, in view of God's mercy, to offer your bodies as living sacrifices, holy and pleasing to God—this is your spiritual act of worship."

In the Old Testament, God condemned formal worship that was not accompanied by a concern for compassion and justice (see Isa. 1:10–17; Mic. 6:6–8). In Hosea 6:6, God says, "For I desire mercy, not sacrifice, and acknowledgment of God rather than burnt offerings." God did, of course, desire sacrifice; this is a rhetorical exaggeration or hyperbole. But the point should not be missed that authentic worship includes a life that is obedient to God.

Therefore, it is not surprising that in the New Testament, the vocabulary of worship takes on a broad, ethical meaning. This is to be expected also because the New Testament regards the temple worship as coming to an end. When Jesus died, the veil of the temple (which separated the people from the presence of God) was torn in two, from top to bottom (Matt. 27:51). And the temple priesthood, based on descent from Aaron, gave way to the eternal priesthood of Christ "after the order of Melchizedek" (Heb. 5:6; 6:20–7:28). In A.D. 70, the temple itself was destroyed. Now, in Christ, all believers are priests, offering spiritual sacrifices (1 Peter 2:5, 9). Those sacrifices include "a sacrifice of praise" (Heb. 13:15), but also "to do good and to share with others" (Heb. 13:16; compare Phil. 4:18). Greed is idolatry (Eph. 5:5; compare Matt. 6:24). The apostle James says,

> If anyone considers himself religious [*threskos*, "observing religious rites"] and yet does not keep a tight rein on

his tongue, he deceives himself and his religion is worth-
less. Religion [*threskeia*] that God our Father accepts as
pure and faultless is this: to look after orphans and wid-
ows in their distress and to keep oneself from being pol-
luted by the world. (James 1:26–27)

This broadly ethical concept of worship I shall sometimes
call "worship in the broad sense." Although it does not consist
of formal rites, it is quite important to the overall biblical concept of worship. We can see already that worship in the narrow
sense without worship in the broad sense is not acceptable to
God.

It is true in one sense to say that all of life is worship. This
is not to deny the importance, indeed the necessity, of attend-
ing church meetings (Heb. 10:25). But our Lord wants us to live
in such a way that everything we do brings him praise.

The Importance of Worship

Worship, as I have defined it, including both broad and narrow
senses, is tremendously important to God. In Ephesians 1:1–14,
the apostle Paul presents a breathtaking vision of God's sovereign purpose. He begins before time: God "chose us in [Christ]
before the creation of the world" (v. 4). Then God "predestined
us to be adopted as his sons" (v. 5), redeemed us through the
blood of Christ (v. 7), and revealed to us the mysteries of his will,
which will be fulfilled at the end of history (vv. 9–10). The conclusion of all, the goal to which all history proceeds, is praise—
the "praise of his glory" (v. 14).

"Man's chief end is to glorify God, and to enjoy him forever," we learn in question 1 of the Westminster Shorter Catechism. This statement of the goal of human life is a scriptural
statement (see 1 Cor. 10:31). But to glorify God is to praise him.[8]
The book of Revelation presents us with a heaven and an earth
filled with praise as the culmination of God's redemption (Rev.
5:13; 7:12).

We have been chosen as God's special people so that we can

"declare the praises of him who called you out of darkness into his wonderful light" (1 Peter 2:9). God has called Gentiles into his body along with believing Jews so that the Gentiles might join in the songs of praise (Rom. 15:8–11).

Throughout the whole Bible story—from eternity past until the new heavens and the new earth—God "seeks" worshipers (John 4:23). It is unusual in Scripture to read of his seeking human beings. Seeking in Scripture is usually done by human beings, not by God. In the usual sense, God never seeks, for there is nothing hidden from his eyes (Heb. 4:13). But the metaphor of seeking is appropriate, for in the Bible we read of God's going to enormous trouble over many centuries, culminating in the sacrifice of his own Son, to redeem a people to worship him.

Redemption is the means; worship is the goal. In one sense, worship is the whole point of everything. It is the purpose of history, the goal of the whole Christian story. Worship is not one segment of the Christian life among others. Worship is the entire Christian life, seen as a priestly offering to God. And when we meet together as a church, our time of worship is not merely a preliminary to something else; rather, it is the whole point of our existence as the body of Christ.

It is therefore important for us to study worship. In evangelical churches, it is widely recognized that we should study evangelism, Bible books and characters, systematic theology, counseling, preaching, and many other things. Too rarely do we consider the importance of studying how our God wants us to worship. Worship is something we tend to take for granted. I trust that this book will help us to grow in our knowledge of the subject and to take the business of worship more seriously.

Questions for Discussion

1. Two basic concepts emerge from the biblical terms translated "worship." What are they? How do they help us to define *worship?*
2. What does it mean to say that God is "Lord"? What are the implications of God's lordship for worship?

3. What are the main differences between worshiping God and honoring human beings?
4. How did Adam's fall into sin affect worship?
5. Should we receive benefits from worship? Should we enjoy it? Should we receive blessings from it? If so, what kind of blessings?
6. How can worship be both God-centered and attentive to human needs? Does the worship of your church need to recover a biblical balance in this area? What changes need to be made to recover that balance?
7. How does the doctrine of the Trinity affect our worship? How does each of the three persons help us to worship God? May we worship together with Jews or Muslims who reject the Trinity?
8. What does it mean to worship "in Spirit and in truth"?
9. Is it true that all of life is worship? Give a biblical basis for your answer. Some people say, "All of life is worship, so I can worship God on the golf course on Sunday morning." Reply.
10. "Sometimes when I'm tired on Sunday morning, I come late to church. I skip the worship and arrive in time for the sermon." Reply.

Notes

[1]Particularly *abodah* in Hebrew and *latreia* in Greek.

[2]*Shachah* in Hebrew and *proskuneo* in Greek.

[3]*Worship Is a Verb* (Waco, Tex.: Word, 1987).

[4]Donald A. Carson, ed., *Worship: Adoration and Action* (Grand Rapids: Baker, 1993).

[5]The concept of covenant lordship has parallels in the secular literature of the ancient Near East. Documents called suzerainty treaties have been found, in which a great king made a treaty with a lesser or vassal king, promising various benefits and demanding from the vassal exclusive loyalty, a loyalty sometimes called love. The vassal was forbidden to conclude any similar treaty with a rival king; he had to serve one king only. The concept of God as covenant Lord is central to the biblical message. For more on the subject, see Meredith G. Kline, *The Structure of Biblical Authority* (Grand Rapids: Eerdmans, 1972) and my

own *The Doctrine of the Knowledge of God* (Phillipsburg, N.J.: Presbyterian and Reformed, 1987).

[6]Ibid., 15–18.

[7]Compare 2 Thess. 2:13: "God chose you to be saved through the sanctifying work of the Spirit and through belief in the truth."

[8]*Doxazo* in the Greek.

2

Worship in the Old Testament

In this chapter and the next, we shall look at the forms of worship described in the Bible. In discussing Old Testament worship, I shall be brief, for the details of Israel's worship are often somewhat difficult to follow, and knowledge of those details is not always important to our decisions about present-day Christian worship. Nevertheless, it is necessary for us to understand the general character and major forms of Israel's worship.

Meetings with God

Frequently in the Old Testament, we read of meetings between God and various people. God spoke to Adam and Eve, both before and after the Fall. He appeared to Noah, Abraham, Jacob, Moses, and many others. When God met with men, the situation was immediately one of worship. When God met with Moses at the burning bush, Moses had to remove his shoes, for he stood on holy ground (Ex. 3:5). He hid his face for fear of God (v. 6). He heard God's word and went forth to carry out his divinely given responsibility (3:7–4:31).

15

Isaiah saw God "seated on a throne, high and exalted, and the train of his robe filled the temple" (Isa. 6:1). God was surrounded by angels uttering praises so loud that they shook the building (vv. 2–4). Isaiah was overwhelmed, not only with the greatness of God, but also because he knew he was a sinner (v. 5). How could a sinner be in the presence of the living God? But God forgave Isaiah's sins through a symbolic atonement: a coal from the altar touched Isaiah's lips (v. 7). Then God called Isaiah to be a prophet (vv. 8–13).

These meetings were very different from one another, but there were important similarities between them. God appeared in his majesty as the Lord. The worshiper was filled with reverential fear. The Lord's control, authority, and presence were much in evidence. His might and power were overwhelming, he spoke a word of authority, and he revealed himself in the presence of the worshiper. The worshiper did not remain the same. He went forth with a new commission, to serve God in a new way.

On one occasion, and only one, God met with the entire nation of Israel. After God had met and commissioned Moses, Moses told Pharaoh, the king of Egypt, to let the people of Israel leave Egypt, that they might worship him at a festival, offering sacrifices (Ex. 5:1–3). They did not leave until after God had sent plagues on the Egyptians. But from the beginning, they knew that they were leaving Egypt in order to meet with God. And God did meet with them on Mount Sinai (Ex. 19–20:21). Like Isaiah's meeting with God, the Mount Sinai experience was terrifying. Israel saw an awesome display of God's power and presence, and they heard a terrifying word, the Ten Commandments, which convicted them of sin. Their response was to say to Moses, "Speak to us yourself and we will listen. But do not have God speak to us or we will die" (Ex. 20:19). God honored their request.

One sometimes hears Christians express the wish that they could speak with God personally, as he appeared to people during the biblical period. But meetings with God in the Bible are awesome and terrible. Job also requested an interview with God (see Job 23:1–7; 31:35–37). But the interview God granted him was terrifying and humiliating (see chaps. 38–42). Perhaps we should be satisfied, even thankful, that our meetings with God today are less direct (though just as real, as we shall see). Surely we can be thankful that we stand before God in Christ, who has borne the fearsome wrath of God in our place.

Spontaneous Worship

Although, as we shall see, God set aside special times for worship, it could take place at any time and at any place. Scripture speaks of private prayer (Dan. 6:10; Matt. 6:6) and family teaching (Deut. 6:4–9). When Moses returned to Egypt after meeting God, and told the Israelites God's promise to deliver them, "they bowed down and worshiped" (Ex. 4:31). The Psalms are full of prayer to God in the midst of difficult situations and praise to him in response to deliverance. Worship is something natural to God's people. As God is Lord of all of life, every experience of life reveals him in some way. And as we recognize God's presence in our lives, the natural response is prayer and praise.

Worship, therefore, need not be organized and scheduled to be valid. Nevertheless, in the Scriptures God does organize and schedule the worship of his people in a wide variety of ways, as we shall see in the following sections.

Covenantal Worship

Central to Israel's worship was the consciousness that they were the special people of God, chosen from among all the nations to be God's own people. The root meaning of *holy* is "separate," and therefore Israel, which was separated from all other nations, was God's "holy" people. This does not necessarily mean that Israel was more faithful to God than other nations were. But at least they were different, and God told them to display that difference in their conduct.

Holiness is a liturgical concept, part of worship. Since Israel was God's holy people, Israel's very existence was worship. The whole life of the nation was worship, set apart to God. In this way,

Scripture introduces us to the concept of worship in the broad sense.

Therefore, the Law of Moses directed every area of Israel's life, not just those things we normally call "religious." It contained rules for prayer and sacrifice; it exhorted Israel to hear and obey God's word, to sing praises to him, and to perform various rites. But it also directed the civil government in its penalties for various crimes. It governed the calendar of the people, and their family life, sexual relationships, economic system, diet, and cycle of work and rest. God's law ruled every aspect of human life.

Many ordinances of the law served mainly to reinforce the distinction between Israel and the other nations. Israelites were to wear distinctive garments, to avoid foods that the pagans ate, and so on. The fundamental distinguishing sign was circumcision. Full access to temple worship was available only to those who were circumcised.

Sacrificial Worship

Shortly after the fall of the human race, people began bringing offerings to the Lord. Cain and Abel brought offerings to God (Gen. 4:2–5). After the Flood, Noah built an altar and sacrificed "clean animals and clean birds" to the Lord (Gen. 8:20–22). On that occasion, God made a covenant with Noah. Later, animals were also sacrificed as God made a covenant with Abraham (Gen. 15). The Lord, in a fiery appearance, passed between the pieces of cut-up animals, promising that Abraham's descendants would possess the land of Palestine.

God later made a covenant with the people of Israel under the leadership of Moses. This covenant included an elaborate system of offerings of animals, grains, wine, oil, and incense. There were offerings for the whole nation: daily, weekly (on the Sabbath), monthly (the new moon), and at the annual feasts (Num. 28–29). There were offerings made by individuals for sin, consecration, and communion with God (Lev. 1–7). The offering for communion—the "peace offering" or "fellowship offering"—

was partially eaten by the worshiper and the priests as a meal of fellowship with God. There were also offerings on special occasions, such as the making of covenants, the consecration of priests, and the dedication of the temple.

The sacrifices did not atone for Israel's sin, for "it is impossible for the blood of bulls and goats to take away sins" (Heb. 10:4). Their purpose was to point ahead in time to Jesus, the Lamb of God, as the one who would offer himself as the final sacrifice for sins.

Sabbaths

The fourth of the Ten Commandments requires Israel to "remember the Sabbath day by keeping it holy" (Ex. 20:8). To keep a day holy is in itself an act of worship. In this case, the holiness of the day was observed by a cessation of work, by sacrificial offerings, and by "sacred assembly" (Lev. 23:3). The Sabbath was not something new when God gave the Ten Commandments to Israel. Exodus 20:11 teaches that God gave the Sabbath to man at his creation, and that we should imitate the pattern of God's creative activity: six days of work and one of rest.

In Israel's law, however, the weekly Sabbath became part of a system of Sabbaths. There were special Sabbath days in addition to the weekly Sabbath during the observance of Passover and other special occasions (note, for example, Lev. 23:7). God also commanded Israel to observe a sabbatical year: every seventh year the land was to "rest," to lie fallow (Lev. 25:1–7). In the fiftieth year, the year following the seventh sabbatical year, another sabbatical year occurred, the Jubilee, during which property that had been sold reverted to the family of the original owner (Lev. 25:8–13).

Feasting

Three times a year, all Israelite males were expected to go to a central location (eventually Jerusalem) for divinely appointed feasts (see Lev. 23). The double Feast of Passover and Unleavened Bread was celebrated in our month of March or April, remembering the Lord's deliverance of Israel from Egypt and the covenant by which Israel as a nation became God's people. The Feast of Pentecost (also called the Feast of Weeks, or Firstfruits), in May or June, celebrated the wheat harvest. Later tradition regarded Pentecost, held fifty days after Passover, as the anniversary of God's meeting with Israel at Mount Sinai and of the giving of the law. The Feast of Tabernacles in the fall, preceded by a two-week period that included the Feast of Trumpets and the Day of Atonement, marked the completion of the harvest and commemorated Israel's wanderings in the wilderness. The people gathered in Jerusalem were to live in booths or tents, reminding themselves of the rigors of the journey. At the Feast of Trumpets, the law was read, and on the Day of Atonement, sins were confessed. Following the public confession, the high priest entered the Most Holy Place in the tabernacle or the temple, the seat of the divine presence, bearing blood for his own sin and the sins of the people.

Tabernacle and Temple

Through Moses, God commanded Israel to build him a place in which he would "dwell among them" (Ex. 25:8). Exodus 25–28 records God's detailed instructions for building the structure. Israel was to "make this tabernacle and all its furnishings exactly like the pattern I will show you" (25:9; compare v. 40; Heb. 8:5). Bezalel and Oholiab, the craftsmen who supervised the construction, were chosen by God and filled with the Holy Spirit to perform their task (Ex. 31:1–3).

The tabernacle itself was a kind of tent, enclosed in a rectangular courtyard. In the courtyard, 150 by 75 feet, was the altar of burnt offering and a basin (or laver) for the priests' ceremonial washings. The tabernacle itself was divided into two rooms, the Holy Place and the Most Holy Place, which were separated by a curtain. In the Holy Place was the table for the bread of the Presence, a lampstand, and the altar of incense. In the Most Holy Place was the ark of the covenant—the throne or seat of the divine presence. With the ark were kept the two stone tablets on which were written the Ten Commandments, a golden pot full of the manna by which God miraculously fed Israel in the wilderness, and Aaron's staff that budded miraculously, confirming Aaron and his sons as Israel's priests (Num. 17:1–13). No one could enter the Most Holy Place except the high priest, and he only once a year on the Day of Atonement.

The tabernacle was, of course, portable, as was appropriate to Israel's period of wilderness wandering. By the time of King David, however, God expressed his desire for a more permanent dwelling place. David himself was not permitted to build the new structure, for he, a man of war, had shed much human blood. David's son Solomon carried out the task according to plans that the Spirit of God had given to David (1 Chron. 28). The plan of the temple was similar to that of the tabernacle, but the temple was much larger and was constructed with nonportable materials. The furniture was the same, but there was more of it: ten golden lampstands, ten tables for the bread of the Presence, and ten basins (2 Chron. 4).

The temple was destroyed three times and rebuilt twice. The "second temple" was built after the Exile; the temple that existed during Jesus' earthly ministry was built by Herod the Great. The tabernacle, and even more the temple, were beautifully decorated, full of precious metals and other materials.

The tabernacle and the temple were largely devoted to sacrificial worship. But they were also places for prayer (1 Kings 8:22–53; Isa. 56:7; Matt. 21:13; Acts 3:1), swearing of oaths (1 Kings 8:22–53), singing of praise (1 Chron. 15:16–22; 25:1–31), and teaching (Matt. 26:55; Luke 2:41–52; Acts 5:21).

Priests and Levites

Levi was one of the twelve tribes of Israel, descended from the son of Jacob by that name, the tribe to which Moses and Aaron belonged. But unlike the other tribes, the Levites did not receive one of the twelve divisions of territory in the Promised Land. God was their inheritance (Num. 18:20–24; Deut. 10:9; 12:12).

He gave them a special assignment, the "care of the sanctuary and the altar" (Num. 18:5). For this service they received the tithes given by all the other tribes (Num. 18:21). This care included relatively menial tasks, but King David also employed Levites as singers and players of instruments for the worship of the sanctuary (1 Chron. 15:16–24; 16:4–6, 37–42).

The Levites were also teachers of God's law (Deut. 33:10; 2 Chron. 17:7–9), and not only at the sanctuary. They were given cities in the territory of the other tribes in which to live and pasture their livestock (Josh. 21). Therefore, although many of them lived near the sanctuary, others were located at various places throughout the land and ministered there.

The priests were a special group of Levites, descended not only from Levi, but from Moses' brother Aaron as well. The priests offered sacrifices at the tabernacle and the temple and took charge of the worship. In effect, they served as mediators between God and Israel, representing the people before God, and God before the people. They also taught the law of God (Lev. 10:10–11), judged questions of ceremonial uncleanness (Lev. 13–15), and handled some civil matters.

The Synagogue

By the time of Jesus' earthly ministry, there were synagogues throughout Palestine and at other places with Jewish populations. A synagogue could be formed by any ten male Jews above twelve years of age. Services were held on the Sabbath and other days of the week. No animals or other offerings were sacrificed at the synagogue; sacrificial worship was restricted to the temple. The synagogue service was a meeting for prayer and study of the Scriptures. Scripture could be read by any male Jew, and the text would be explained and applied to the congregation. There were various prescribed recitations, prayers, benedictions, and congregational responses.

The origins of the synagogue are obscure. Although the Law of Moses gives detailed instructions concerning the worship of the tabernacle and the temple, it mentions nothing about a synagogue meeting. I suspect that even before the Exile, perhaps even from the time of Moses, there was, in addition to the tabernacle worship, some sort of teaching ministry that eventually was dispersed throughout the land. I mentioned earlier that the Levites who lived at a distance from the sanctuary had teaching responsibilities in their own communities. Second Kings 4:23 implies that believers in the northern kingdom were accustomed to visiting "men of God" on Sabbaths and new moons. Another indication of such an institution is that Leviticus 23:3 connects the Sabbath with a "sacred assembly," without describing further what is to take place at that weekly meeting. Some sort of Sabbath service, initially convened by Levites—perhaps held first near the tabernacle, but later at various points throughout the land—may well in time have developed into what we now know as the synagogue. The destruction of the temple and the exile of the Jews doubtless made this type of meeting all the more important.

Following the Exile, Israel's leaders saw the teaching of Scripture to be of the highest priority for the restoration of Israel as God's people in the Promised Land. Jewish tradition cites Ezra as the founder of the synagogue. The long meeting at which he taught the law of God (Neh. 8–9) is sometimes known as the "Great Synagogue."

Jesus attended the synagogue regularly and taught there (Luke 4:15–16), so there can be no question as to God's approval of the institution. It is interesting, however, to note that the synagogue and the temple were very different in their scriptural warrant: God regulated the sacrificial worship of the tabernacle and the temple in detail, charging the people to do everything strictly according to the revealed pattern. He hardly said anything to Israel, however, about the synagogue (or, for that matter, about the ministries of teaching and prayer carried out on the temple grounds), leaving the arranging of its services largely to the discretion of the people. Of course, they knew in general what God wanted: he wanted his word to be taught and prayer to be offered. But God left the specifics open-ended.

It is even an open question whether the synagogue meeting should be called "worship." In the Old Testament, the worship vocabulary typically refers to the sacrificial offerings of the tabernacle and the temple, which did not take place in the synagogue. However, those who attended the synagogue did pay homage to God, and homage is one defining feature of worship, as I indicated in the previous chapter. And if the synagogue meeting was the sacred assembly of Leviticus 23:3, then it was clearly a meeting with God and therefore a time of worship.

Conclusion

There were many different kinds of worship in the Old Testament period. There were meetings between God and man, spontaneous prayers, prescribed sacrifices, a calendar of regular worship events at different intervals, beautiful buildings for worship, divinely instituted leadership for sacrificial worship, and the teaching of God's word.

Questions for Discussion

1. "Whenever God meets with man, the situation becomes one of worship." Explain.
2. Why does the Old Testament place so much emphasis on sacrifice, even though it is "impossible for the blood of bulls and goats to take away sins"?
3. Can Old Testament worship properly function without a temple, without provision for sacrifice? How should we evaluate modern Jewish worship in that respect?
4. How is Christian worship like and unlike the worship of the temple? How is it like and unlike the worship of the synagogue? How are Christian pastors like and unlike Old Testament priests and Levites? Compare the Lord's Supper to the "fellowship offering" and the Passover.
5. Why was God so insistent in telling the people to follow precisely his revealed directions for building the tabernacle? Why, then, did he give them so little information as to how he wanted them to conduct the synagogue meeting?

3

Worship in the New Testament

Christ Fulfills Old Testament Worship

The most significant fact about worship in the New Testament is that its focus is on Jesus. As I indicated in chapter 1, Jesus comes as the Lord of the covenant. He displays the control, authority, and presence that Yahweh associated with his own lordship over Israel. He brings to his people a deliverance greater than the Old Testament deliverance from Egyptian slavery—he delivers his people from their sin. He makes them into a new people of God (see 1 Peter 2:9), encompassing Jew and Gentile in one body to give him worship.

From a New Testament perspective, we can see all the various elements of Old Testament worship pointing to Jesus. In him we meet with God (John 1:14). His death for sin and his glorious resurrection move us to spontaneous praise. For example, the apostle Paul, over and over again, pauses in his descriptions of Christ's work to give joyful praise to the Lord (see Rom. 9:5; 11:33–36; Eph. 1:15–23; 3:14–21).

Jesus is the ultimate sacrifice for sin and therefore brings an end to the temple offerings of bulls and goats (Heb. 10:1–18; Eph. 5:2; Mark 10:45). The Old Testament sacrifices had to be made every day, over and over again, which showed their insufficiency to take away sin. But Jesus' sacrifice of himself on the cross dealt with sin "once for all." His sacrifice suffices to make his people holy (Heb. 10:10).

Jesus is also the one who *brings* the ultimate sacrifice; that is to say, he is the ultimate priest. Being both God and man, he is the ultimate mediator—the only such mediator—between God and man (1 Tim. 2:5). The book of Hebrews (6:13–8:13) calls Jesus a priest, not after the order of Aaron, but after the order of Melchizedek, the mysterious priest who "brought out bread and wine" to Abraham, and to whom Abraham presented tithes (Gen. 14:18–20). In the Genesis narrative, Melchizedek appears out of nowhere, without genealogy and with nothing said of his life before or after his meeting with Abraham. Similarly, says the writer to the Hebrews, Jesus is not connected with the tribe of Levi or the sons of Aaron. He begins a whole new priesthood, "not on the basis of a regulation as to his ancestry but on the basis of the power of an indestructible life" (7:16). And his priesthood is permanent because he "lives forever" (7:24). Unlike the Aaronic priests, he does not lose his office because of death. "Therefore he is able to save completely those who come to God through him, because he always lives to intercede for them" (7:25).

Hebrews also tells us that Jesus, as the ultimate high priest, ministers at a tabernacle that is far greater than the tabernacle or the temple of the Old Testament. Recall from chapter 2 that God required Israel's tabernacle to be built precisely in accordance with a detailed plan revealed by God. I asked why that should be, in view of the fact that God revealed no specific regulations for the synagogue. In Hebrews 8:1–6 we learn the reason: the earthly tabernacle was to be, as much as possible, a copy of the tabernacle in heaven. The heavenly tabernacle is the ultimate dwelling of God's presence. For us to enjoy eternal fellowship with God, our sins must be dealt with in that eternal tabernacle. Jesus, as the ultimate high priest, brought his own blood to the heavenly tabernacle as the one perfect and permanent sacrifice for sin (see 9:11–28).

In a somewhat different use of the symbols, Jesus himself *is* God's tabernacle and temple. He is the one in whom God tabernacled with his people (John 1:14). After Jesus cast out the salesmen from the temple at Jerusalem, the Jews asked him for a miraculous sign of his authority.

> Jesus answered them, "Destroy this temple, and I will raise it again in three days." The Jews replied, "It has taken forty-six years to build this temple, and you are going to raise it in three days?" But the temple he had spoken of was his body. After he was raised from the dead, his disciples recalled what he had said. Then they believed the Scripture and the words that Jesus had spoken. (John 2:19–22)

Jesus is God's dwelling among men. The purpose of the temple was to point forward to him. In the final consummation of history, the "New Jerusalem," there will be no temple, for "the Lord God Almighty and the Lamb are its temple" (Rev. 21:22).

Therefore, all the tabernacle and temple furniture speak of Christ (Heb. 9:1–5). The altar of burnt offering speaks of his sacrifice of himself. The basin, like the sacrament of baptism, speaks of Christ as the priest who is perfectly clean, free from any defilement, and who cleanses his people. The lampstand represents Christ as the light of the world. The bread of the Presence and the manna, like the sacrament of the Lord's Supper, present Christ as the one who feeds his people. The altar of incense and Aaron's rod represent Christ as the priest whose prayers for his people always ascend to the Father's throne. The Most Holy Place was opened to us at the death of Christ, when the veil of the temple was torn in two. Through Christ, we enter boldly (Heb. 10:19–25). The ark, God's throne in Israel, represents Jesus as "God with us," Immanuel. The tablets of the law speak of Christ as God's eternal Word.

Jesus is also "Lord of the Sabbath" (Matt. 12:8),[1] and the focal point of the annual feasts. He is the Passover lamb (John 1:29; 1 Cor. 5:7). He is the one who sends his Spirit on Pentecost to empower the church. He fulfills the Day of Atonement by bringing the ultimate blood-sacrifice to God in the Most Holy Place. He embodies the Feast of Tabernacles, as he dwells forever with his people in human flesh. John 1:14 says, "The Word became flesh and made his dwelling [literally, "tabernacled"] among us."

Jesus is also the true Israel, the faithful remnant of God's people. Those who are in him are the new Israel, the "Israel of God" (Gal. 6:16), the heirs of God's promises to Abraham. Christians, therefore, worship God in the consciousness that they are God's elect, God's people, chosen in Christ before the foundation of the world (Eph. 1:4). Like Israel at Mount Sinai, we have assembled in God's presence. But just as the earthly tabernacle was an image of a far greater tabernacle in heaven, so the assembly at Sinai was an image of a far greater assembly in heaven. We are part of that greater assembly.

> But you have come to Mount Zion, to the heavenly Jerusalem, the city of the living God. You have come to thousands upon thousands of angels in joyful assembly, to the church of the firstborn, whose names are written in heaven. You have come to God, the judge of all men, to the spirits of righteous men made perfect, to Jesus the mediator of a new covenant, and to the sprinkled blood that speaks a better word than the blood of Abel. (Heb. 12:22–24)

We also have a greater circumcision, separating us from all the nations of the earth as God's holy people. Against those who insisted that Christians must be circumcised, Paul replies, "For it is we who are the circumcision, we who worship by the Spirit of God, who glory in Christ Jesus, and who put no confidence in the flesh" (Phil. 3:3).

In Christ we are not only the true Israel, but also priests. As he is the ultimate high priest, we are all called to be his priestly people (1 Peter 2:5, 9; Rev. 1:6; 5:10; 20:6). In the New Testament church, there is no special group of priests, as in Old Testament

Israel. Rather, we all bring to God "spiritual" sacrifices of praise, prayer, godly behavior, and our whole existence (Rom. 12:1; Phil. 2:17; 4:18; Heb. 13:15–16).

We are not only priests, but also temples. Our bodies are temples of the Holy Spirit (1 Cor. 6:19). For this reason, Paul teaches, they should not be defiled by sexual sin. Or, to put it somewhat differently, the church as a whole is God's temple, not to be defiled by division or pride (1 Cor. 3:16–17; 2 Cor. 6:19; Eph. 2:21). But it is only "in him" (in Christ) that we are joined to one another as a holy temple. We are a temple only insofar as we are the body of Christ.

Clearly, then, Christian worship should be full of Christ. We come to the Father only by him (John 14:6). In worship we look to him as our all-sufficient Lord and Savior. Christ must be inescapably prominent and pervasive in every occasion of Christian worship.

Worship in the Broad Sense

The great changes from the Old Testament to the New imply that there will be changes in worship. As the new Israel in Christ, the church worships in a way that is parallel to that of the Old Testament, in that every ordinance of the Old Testament is fulfilled in Christ. We too have a covenant, a priesthood, sacrifices, a tabernacle, circumcision, atonement, and feasts. But in our actual practice, there are great differences, for all of these institutions now exist in Christ and in him alone. And our worship in Christ presupposes the once-for-all accomplishment of the redemption to which the Old Testament Jews looked forward.

One difference that should already be evident is that in the New Testament, the traditional terminology for worship is typically used in the broad sense. That is to be expected. The literal temple is no more; there are no more animal sacrifices; there is no more Aaronic priesthood. Circumcision and the annual feasts are no longer required. We appreciate all of these ordinances for their witness to Christ, but once he has come and accomplished redemption, there is no further need for their literal observance. Indeed, the literal observance of these rites would distract us from the final accomplishment of salvation in Jesus. Therefore, God no longer requires our participation in these ceremonies. But what is left when these ceremonies are no longer required? Essentially, what is left is worship in the broad sense: a life of obedience to God's word, a sacrifice of ourselves to his purposes. All of life is our priestly service, our homage to the greatness of our covenant Lord.

Christian Meetings

But this fact should not be taken to imply that there is no New Testament mandate for corporate praise and prayer, teaching and sacrament, or meetings in which God draws near to his people in a special way. Clearly, there were such meetings among the early Christians—meetings sanctioned by the apostles as Jesus' representatives.

Jesus promises a special blessing—indeed, his special presence—upon his people when they are gathered in his name (Matt. 18:20;[2] compare John 14:13–14, 26; 16:23–26). The Lord's Supper is not like other meals; it is, in some mysterious way, "a participation in the blood of Christ" and "a participation in the body of Christ" (1 Cor. 10:16). The bread and the wine must be taken in a worthy manner (1 Cor. 11:27), for Jesus called it "the new covenant in my blood" (v. 25).

From the beginning of the New Testament church, believers delighted in meeting together, and in those meetings they experienced unique blessings of the Spirit of God (Acts 1:6, 14; 2:42–47; 4:23–31; 5:42; 13:2; 20:7–38; 1 Cor. 11:18–34; 14:1–40; 1 Peter 3:21). They met for prayer, teaching, and sacrament. They pronounced publicly in the meeting the judgments of church discipline (1 Cor. 5:4–5). The church received gifts for Christians in special need (1 Cor. 16:1–2). They exchanged the "holy kiss" (Rom. 16:16; 1 Cor. 16:20).

By the Spirit of God, supernatural events took place. There were utterances in languages unknown to the speaker, God-given interpretations of those utterances, and divinely inspired prophecies in familiar languages (1 Cor. 14:1–25). In my opinion, these supernatural gifts were given to the church only for the period of its founding, to attest the ministry of the apostles (Heb. 2:1–4; 2 Cor. 12:12; Eph. 2:20).[3] That ministry is available to us in the Scriptures, and so we should not expect God to give these gifts to us today.

Nevertheless, it cannot be doubted that in the permanent aspects of New Testament meetings, as well as the temporary extraordinary aspects, God is present in a special way in the Christian meeting. When Christians worship as God commands them to, even an unbeliever will be driven to worship, recognizing that "God is really among you!" (1 Cor. 14:25).

For this reason, the meeting is not something optional. Many professing Christians today believe that they can go to church or not as they please. They will go if they are not tired, or busy with something else, or working, or socializing, or watching a football game. For them, the meeting itself has a very low priority. Usually this behavior is unthinking and therefore unworthy of Christians. But when such people do try to relate their behavior to the word of God, they sometimes reason that true piety is in all of life, not in meetings, and that they can worship God perfectly well in their own living rooms or on the golf course. But the writer to the Hebrews has a very different view. To him the meeting is vitally important: "Let us not give up meeting together, as some are in the habit of doing, but let us encourage one another—and all the more as you see the Day approaching" (Heb. 10:25).

Is the Christian meeting a "worship service"? Some have said no, on the ground that in the New Testament all of life is worship.[4] It is true that the New Testament does not describe the early Christians as meeting for "worship." Nor does the New Testament typically use the Old Testament language of sacrifice and priesthood to describe the Christian meeting as such. Much of the New Testament teaching about the meeting has a horizontal focus: the importance of showing love for one another in the meetings (1 Cor. 11–14), the importance of edification (1 Cor. 14:26; Heb. 10:24–25).

Nevertheless, we have seen that in the meeting, God draws

near to his people in a special way. It is hard to define that "special way" precisely. God is, of course, omnipresent, so he is always near to us (Ps. 139). That fact, of course, is relevant to worship in the broad sense—all the earth is God's temple.

Throughout redemptive history, however, God has, from time to time, made his presence particularly overwhelming and intense. Something very unusual and important happened when Moses met God in the burning bush, when Israel met God at Sinai, and when the glory of God descended on the tabernacle. And something similar happens when God draws near to the New Testament Christian meeting, even though there may be no visual spectacle, as there often was in the Old Testament. When Christians meet in the name of Christ, the gathering is not merely worship in the broad sense, though it certainly is that. Something more is happening, and it deserves a special name.

Traditionally, Christians have called it "worship," having in mind a sense of the term that is analogous to its use in the temple setting. This use of the worship vocabulary is somewhat dangerous, for it may lead us to forget the vast differences that exist between Old Testament temple worship and the New Testament meeting. But there are certainly similarities as well as differences, and our terminology must take both into account.

Terminological questions are never matters of life and death. Modern English is different from Old Testament Hebrew and New Testament Greek, and it is rarely possible to achieve a perfect correspondence between an English expression and the expressions found in the Bible's original languages. Often we need many English words to express the various nuances of one Greek term, or vice versa. A good translator must struggle, considering many possibilities, to find the best rendering. Accordingly, we may describe the New Testament meeting as "worship," as long as we use other terms to differentiate between the different kinds of worship. Or, we can withhold the term *worship* from the Christian meeting—but then we must find other terminology to express the divine presence in the meeting and the special homage given there to God.

I have sometimes used this illustration: Imagine that you are working in a king's palace, scrubbing floors. Despite the menial character of your job, you have a special feeling about being there. You are loyal to the king, and you admire him. And you do your work, after all, in the king's palace. At work, in a real sense, you are in the king's presence, and all your labors are a service, a kind of homage, to him. But every now and then something special happens: you find yourself talking to the king himself. It may be that he merely passes by and makes a casual remark, or you may attend some official meeting. In either case, when this happens, your service takes on a different character. The occasion—even a casual meeting—becomes somewhat ceremonial. You bow, and you remember as best you can the language of homage: "Your Majesty." As a good servant, you seek in various ways to express respect for your master and to express support for his purposes.

The illustration isn't perfect, since God is not physical, and his "drawing near" is not always visible. But something like this happens in our relation to God. All of life is worship, in that we always seek to serve our Lord and to pay him homage. All the world is his palace (Isa. 66:1). But when he meets with us, something special happens. The Bible uses the term "worship" to express that special situation, even apart from the priestly ministry of the tabernacle and the temple. Recall the spontaneous worship recorded in passages like Exodus 4:31. Recall the solemn awe of Abraham, Jacob, and Isaiah when God met with them.

Furthermore, although Scripture doesn't speak specifically of the Christian meeting as a worship service, it does use worship terminology for some things that we do at the meeting. Our gifts can be "a fragrant offering, an acceptable sacrifice, pleasing to God" (Phil. 4:18; compare Heb. 13:16). Our praises are sacrifices (Heb. 13:15; compare Hos. 14:2). Prayers in Scripture are often closely related to the smoke that arose from the altar of incense in the tabernacle and the temple (Ps. 141:2; Luke 1:10; Rev. 5:8; 8:3–4). Prayer is a lifting up of "holy hands" (1 Tim. 2:8). The word that we read and preach is "holy" (Rom. 7:12; 2 Tim. 3:16; 2 Peter 2:21; 3:2). In Hebrews 4:12, that word pierces into our inmost parts: the language is that of sacrifice. The kiss by which

New Testament Christians expressed their fellowship and unity was also "holy" (Rom. 16:16; 1 Cor. 16:20; 2 Cor. 13:12; 1 Thess. 5:26). We, as the church, are a holy temple (1 Cor. 3:17; Eph. 2:21; 5:27; Rev. 21:2, 10) and a holy priesthood (1 Peter 2:5). In worship, we draw near to the heavenly Jerusalem, to God and the angels in joyful assembly (Heb. 12:22–24).

Therefore, it is not wrong to describe the Christian meeting as, in one sense, a worship service. To say this, however, is not to say that there is a sharp distinction between what we do in the meeting and what we do outside of it. Our holiness, our priesthood, our incense-prayers, and our obedient hearing of the Holy Book are not restricted to the church meetings. The difference between worship in the broader sense and worship in the narrower sense is a difference in degree. All the earth is God's temple. As in the case of the palace worker, there is a sense in which we are always in God's presence, always meeting with him. On various occasions, however, God seems to draw nearer. What the New Testament teaches is that when God's people meet together in the name of Jesus, God actually does draw nearer. That is true, whether we feel God's nearness or not. It is his promise, and we should rely on it.

What does "draw near" mean in this context? I have said that it is hard to define, but let me try to clarify the idea somewhat. When God draws near, he has special business with us. As in Isaiah's case, he wants to remind us of his greatness and holiness. He wants us to acknowledge that greatness in our praises. He wants to convict us of sin, and he wants us to confess that sin and receive his forgiveness. He wants us to hear his word and obey it. He wants to hear our baptismal and membership vows, and to preside at the discipline of the church. He wants to fellowship with us in the Lord's Supper. He wants to receive our gifts. He wants us to acknowledge our unity and love for one another as his body. For such purposes, God draws near. And from such fellowship with God in the name of Christ, we arise, empowered by his Spirit, to do his bidding.

When God draws near, we may be greatly blessed. Good things happen. It is also true, however, that God sometimes draws near in judgment (see Gen. 3:8–19; Joel 2:11; Mal. 3:1–5; Matt. 25:31–46; 2 Thess. 2:8). Those who disobey his word, and who do not pay him proper homage, are terrified when God approaches. All of us have offended him; we can only be thankful and amazed that in Christ he has spared us. Not all will be so spared. Of course, the final judgment will not come until the end of history. Therefore, in our worship today, God does not draw near to us in final judgment. But he does reprove sin in the preaching of the word and in the discipline of the church. And those reproofs are particularly intense when God's people are meeting in his name. Consider again 1 Corinthians 14:24–25, in which, as we have seen, an unbeliever visiting the Christian meeting is convinced of sin and worships God, "exclaiming, 'God is really among you!' "

What does it mean to meet in the name of Christ? It simply means meeting because of him, meeting for purposes that arise out of our common commitment to Jesus.

When we meet thus in his name, he meets with us. His name is great and powerful. In Jesus' name his disciples prophesied and worked miracles (Matt. 7:22; Luke 9:49; Acts 3:6; 4:7). For that name, his people have been persecuted (Matt. 10:22; 24:9). In Jesus' name we are baptized (Matt. 28:19; Acts 2:38). In that name we show love to the poor (Mark 9:41). Saving faith is belief in Jesus' name (John 1:12; 3:18; 20:31; Acts 3:16). In his name we pray, and he promises to answer (John 14:13–14, 26; 15:16, 21; 16:23–26). There is no other name by which we must be saved (Acts 4:12).

The name of Christ is inseparable from Christ himself. To praise his name is to praise him. To baptize into his name is to baptize into Christ (Gal. 3:27). To believe in his name is to believe in him.

It is in that wonderful name that we meet. Truly, we should expect much from worship.

Questions for Discussion

1. What are some of the ways in which Jesus fulfills the worship of the Old Testament?

2. Is Christ really central, preeminent, and pervasive in the worship of your church? Why or why not? What can you do to make that worship more Christ-centered?

3. Why is the broad meaning of *worship* especially prominent in the New Testament?

4. Why should you go to church? What do you miss if you don't go? What do others miss if you don't go? Can't you worship God as easily somewhere else, since all of life is worship? Is the service an option or a necessity? Should the church discipline members who do not regularly attend services?

5. Is the Christian meeting a "worship service"? What difference does it make?

6. What does it mean for God to "draw near" to us? What is the difference between the way he draws near to us in worship and the way he draws near to us at other times?

7. What does it mean to meet "in the name of Christ"?

Notes

[1]This phrase is a remarkable testimony to Jesus' deity. The Sabbath was God's holy day, a day separated to him from the other days of the week. God alone was "Lord of the Sabbath."

[2]The immediate context of this verse deals with church discipline, and thus it is an important promise for those churches that faithfully discipline their members according to the whole teaching of Matt. 18. However, in vv. 19 and 20 the purview of the passage becomes broader, dealing with all occasions when believers gather in Jesus' name. Therefore, the promise of v. 20 applies to all meetings of believers in the name of Christ.

[3]See, for example, Anthony A. Hoekema, *What About Tongue-Speaking?* (Grand Rapids: Eerdmans, 1966); Richard B. Gaffin, Jr., *Perspectives on Pentecost* (Phillipsburg, N.J.: Presbyterian and Reformed, 1979).

[4]See David Peterson, "Worship in the New Testament," in *Worship: Adoration and Action,* ed. Donald Carson (Grand Rapids: Baker, 1993), 82–83. Glenn Davies has argued this thesis in detail, in "New Covenant Worship" (Th.M. thesis, Westminster Theological Seminary, 1979). See also Herman Ridderbos, *Paul* (Grand Rapids: Eerdmans, 1975), 481, a well-balanced discussion of this issue.

4

The Rules for Worship

We Need to Know the Rules

It often surprises people to learn that God is not always pleased when people worship him. We might be inclined to think that God should be thankful for any attention we give him out of our busy schedules. But worship is not about God's thanking us; it is about our thanking him. And God is not pleased with just anything we choose to do in his presence. The mighty Lord of heaven and earth demands that our worship—indeed, all of life—be governed by his word.

As early as Genesis 4, we learn that God "did not look with favor" on Cain and his offering (v. 5). In Leviticus 10:1–3, God destroys Aaron's sons Nadab and Abihu because they "offered unauthorized fire before the LORD, contrary to his command." (See also 1 Sam. 13:7–14; 2 Sam. 6:6–7 [compare 1 Chron. 13:9–14; 15:11–15]; 1 Kings 12:32–33; 15:30; 2 Chron. 26:16–23; 28:3; Jer. 7:31; 1 Cor. 11:29–30.)

The first four of the Ten Commandments deal with worship in various ways. They regulate our dealings with the holy. The first forbids the worship of false gods. The second forbids the worship of any god (even the true God) by means of idols. The third forbids wrong uses of God's holy name. The fourth requires us to remember his holy day. Scripture thus draws sharp lines between true and false worship. Condemnation of idolatry permeates the Bible. (In the New Testament, see Acts 17:16; Rom. 1:21–23; 1 Cor. 10:6–22; 2 Cor. 6:16; Gal. 5:20; 1 Peter 4:3; 1 John 5:21; Rev. 21:8; 22:15.)

Therefore, it is a matter of utmost importance, literally a life-and-death matter, to know how to worship God rightly, according to his will. The wrong kind of worship provokes God's wrath, not his blessing. We may not do anything we please in God's awesome presence. Modern Christians are far too casual about worship. The letter to the Hebrews admonishes us to "worship God acceptably with reverence and awe, for our 'God is a consuming fire' " (Heb. 12:28).

How, then, can we worship God acceptably? That is the crucial question. But before we answer that, we must answer another question, namely, How do we find out how to worship God acceptably? Where do we find the rules for worship?

The Regulative Principle

To all Christians, the basic answer is "Scripture." God rules all human life through his word, and he thus rules worship by Scripture.[1] But *how* do we use Scripture to regulate worship? On this question, different groups of Christians have given different answers.

Roman Catholics, Episcopalians, and Lutherans have taken the position that we may do anything in worship except what Scripture forbids. Here Scripture regulates worship in a negative way—by exercising veto power. Presbyterian and Reformed churches, however, have employed a stronger principle: whatever Scripture does not command is forbidden. Here, Scripture has more than veto power; its function is essentially positive. On this view, Scripture must positively require a practice, if that practice is to be suitable for the worship of God.

The Westminster Confession of Faith (21.1) puts it this way:

> The acceptable way of worshiping the true God is instituted by himself, and so limited by his own revealed will, that he may not be worshiped according to the imaginations and devices of men, or the suggestions of Satan, under any visible representation, or any other way not prescribed in the holy Scripture.

The operative word is "prescribed." Eventually this restriction of worship to what God prescribes became known as the "regulative principle" of Reformed and Presbyterian worship.

This regulative principle reflects a genuine insight into the nature of biblical worship. As we have seen, worship is for God, not ourselves. In worship, we seek to honor him. Therefore, we must seek above all to do what pleases him. To do this, we cannot trust our own imaginations. Nadab and Abihu trusted their own wisdom, and God judged them severely. Can any of us trust ourselves to determine, apart from Scripture, what God does and does not like in worship? Our finitude and sin disqualify us from making such judgments. For such a serious decision—potentially a life-and-death decision—we must seek God's own wisdom, the revelation of his own heart. We must ask the Scriptures what God wants us to do in worship. Then, as we worship, we must do those things—and only those things.

Scripture itself condemns worship that is based only on human ideas: "These people come near to me with their mouth and honor me with their lips, but their hearts are far from me. Their worship of me is made up only of rules taught by men" (Isa. 29:13). This word of God through Isaiah was repeated by Jesus in Matthew 15:8–9 and Mark 7:6–7. Paul in Colossians 2:23 condemns "self-imposed worship," worship unauthorized by God.

Scripture, God's word, is sufficient for our worship, as for all of life. We must not add to it, and we dare not subtract anything from it (Deut. 4:2; 12:29–32; 2 Tim. 3:16–17; Rev. 22:18–19).[2]

Applications

Is there, then, no role for human thought, planning, or decisions, in the worship of God? Obviously there is such a role.
Scripture is silent about many things that we do in worship. It
doesn't tell us when or where to meet on Sunday, whether to sit
on pews or chairs, how long the service should be, which hymns
we may sing, or what text the pastor should preach on. So how
can Scripture be a sufficient rule for worship? Do we not need
human wisdom, in addition to Scripture, to plan our worship?

The Westminster divines, who wrote the Confession of
Faith, dealt with this problem by acknowledging that "there are
some circumstances concerning the worship of God, and government of the church, common to human actions and societies,
which are to be ordered by the light of nature, and Christian prudence, according to the general rules of the Word, which are always to be observed" (1.6). Scripture, they believed, was sufficient
to tell us the basic things we should do in worship. But it does
not give us detailed direction in the area of "circumstances."

What are these "circumstances"? The confession does not
define the term, except to say that they are "common to human
actions and societies." Some of the Puritans and Scottish Presbyterians, trying to further explain this idea, taught that circumstances were secular matters, of no actual religious significance. But surely, in God's world, nothing is purely secular;
nothing is entirely devoid of religious significance. That follows from the fact that in one sense worship is all of life. The
time and place of a meeting, for instance, are not religiously
neutral. Decisions about such matters must be made to the
glory of God. The elders of a church would not be exercising
godly rule if they tried to force all the members to worship at
3:00 A.M.! Decisions about the time and place of worship can
greatly affect the quality of edification (1 Cor. 14:26). Although
it is "common to human actions and societies" to make decisions
about meeting times and places, the decision nevertheless has
religious significance in the context of the church. The divines
understood this, and so they insisted that all these decisions be

made "according to the general rules of the Word." But then, how are we to distinguish circumstances from substantive elements of worship?

Furthermore, there seem to be some matters in worship that are not "common to human actions and societies," concerning which we must use our human judgment. For example, Scripture tells us to pray, but it doesn't tell us what precise words to use in our prayers on every occasion. We must decide what words to use, within the limits of the biblical teachings about prayer. That is a decision of great spiritual importance. It does not seem right to describe this matter as a mere "circumstance." Prayer is not "common to human actions and societies."[3] But in prayer we must use our own judgment within biblical guidelines; if we don't, we will not pray at all.

I agree with the confession that there is room for human judgment in matters that are "common to human actions and societies." But I do not believe that that is the only legitimate sphere of human judgment. In my view, the term best suited to describe the sphere of human judgment is not *circumstance*, but *application*.[4] Typically, Scripture tells us what we should do in general and then leaves us to determine the specifics by our own sanctified wisdom, according to the general rules of the Word. Determining the specifics is what I call "application."

Unlike the term *circumstance*, the term *application* naturally covers both types of examples I have mentioned. Applications include such matters as the time and place of worship: Scripture tells us to meet, but not when and where—so we must use our own judgment. Similarly, Scripture tells us to pray, but does not dictate to us all the specific words we should use—so we need to decide. As you can see, the sphere of application includes some matters that are "common to human actions and societies" and some matters that are not.[5]

The process of application is important not only to worship in the narrow sense, but to worship in the broad sense as well; that is, application is important in all of life's decisions. In all decisions, our task is to apply biblical principles to our life situation. For example, Scripture tells us to honor our parents. It doesn't tell me how often to call my mother or what to buy for her birthday. I must make those decisions by godly application of Scripture to my situation.

In everyday life, I am never free from God's commands. When I am obeying the Lord, everything I do is done in obedience to divine commands. Some commands, of course, are more general; others are more specific. "Do it all for the glory of God" (1 Cor. 10:31) is general; "do this in remembrance of me" (1 Cor. 11:24), referring to the Lord's Supper, is relatively specific. By the process of application, I make the general commands specific and the specific commands more so.

Thus understood, the regulative principle for worship is no different from the principles by which God regulates all of our life. That is to be expected, because, as we have seen, worship *is*, in an important sense, all of life. In both cases, "whatever is not commanded is forbidden"— everything we do must be done in obedience to God's commands. In both cases, application determines the specifics in accordance with the general principles of the word.

Does this interpretation of the regulative principle imply that we may do anything in a worship service that we may do anywhere else in life? Certainly not. For there are differences between what we have called the "broad" and the "narrow" senses of worship, even though those differences are not always precisely definable. The worship service is a public event for particular purposes. For example, Paul tells the Corinthians that they should not treat the Lord's Supper as an ordinary meal (1 Cor. 11:20–34). If some are hungry or thirsty, they should eat at home, not in the church meeting (11:34). In the Lord's Supper, we should not eat until we are sure that everybody has bread and wine (11:20–21). Scripture draws distinctions between different situations, and we should observe those distinctions.

We must also make distinctions of this sort that are implicit, though not explicit, in Scripture. Scripture does not, for example, explicitly forbid juggling exhibitions at worship meetings. But Scripture does set forth the purposes of worship meetings; and entertainment—even though lawful at other times, is not normally consistent with those purposes. We may even say that entertainment, when it is consistent with biblical standards, is a form of "worship in the broad sense." But it is generally inconsistent with the purpose of a worship *meeting.*[6]

But the process of decision making is the same in all situations. Both in church meetings and in other settings, our responsibility is to discover what God has commanded in Scripture, and then to apply his commands to the specifics of the situation.

I am aware that traditional Presbyterian statements of the regulative principle typically draw a much sharper distinction than I have drawn between worship services and the rest of life. The Westminster Confession, for example, states that in all of life we are free from any "doctrines and commandments of men" that are "contrary to" God's word, but that in "matters of faith, or worship," we are also free from doctrines and commandments that are "beside" the word (20.2).

My own formulation does not contradict the confession, but goes beyond it. In my view, we are free from anything "beside" the word, not only in "matters of faith, or worship," but in all other areas of life as well.[7] In all areas of life, we are subject to biblical commands. Scripture alone is "given by inspiration of God to be the rule of faith and life," as the confession indicates (1.2). Human wisdom may never presume to *add* to its commands.[8] The only job of human wisdom is to *apply* those commands to specific situations.

Church Power

In the Presbyterian tradition, the regulative principle has been typically discussed in the context of "church power." Historically, the Puritans and early Scottish Presbyterians were faced with what they considered an oppressive state church, which tried to force them to worship in ways they considered unscriptural. The state church, as they saw it, tried to "impose ceremonies" on them, ceremonies not commanded in Scripture. For them, therefore, the issue of the regulative principle was the issue of church power: what may the church require worshipers to do? And the Puritan-Presbyterian answer was, quite properly, only what Scripture commands.

This position on church power, however, led some theologians to distinguish sharply between worship services that are "formal" or "official" (i.e., sanctioned by the ruling body of the church), and other meetings at which worship takes place, such as family devotions, hymn sings at homes, etc., which are not officially sanctioned. Some have said that the regulative principle properly applied only to the formal or official services, not to other forms of worship.

But that distinction is clearly unscriptural. When Scripture forbids us to worship according to our own imaginations, it is not forbidding that only during official services. The God of Scripture would certainly not approve of people who worshiped him in formal services, but worshiped idols in the privacy of their homes![9]

On the Puritan view, the regulative principle pertains primarily to worship that is officially sanctioned by the church. On this view, in order to show that, say, preaching is appropriate for worship, we must show by biblical commands and examples that God requires preaching in officially sanctioned worship services. It is not enough to show that God approves of preaching in general, or that God is pleased when the word is preached in crowds or informal home meetings. Rather, we must show that preaching is mandated precisely for the formal or official worship service. Unfortunately, it is virtually impossible to prove that anything is divinely required specifically for official services. The New Testament simply does not make that distinction. There are commands to preach the gospel, and there are examples of preaching taking place in public meetings of the church (as Acts 20:7), but these meetings are not specified as formal or official.

I therefore reject the limitation of the regulative principle to official worship services. In my view, the regulative principle in Scripture is not primarily a doctrine about church power and officially sanctioned worship services. It is a doctrine about worship, about all forms of worship. It governs *all* worship, whether formal or informal, individual or corporate, public or private, family or church, broad or narrow. Limiting the doctrine to officially sanctioned worship robs it of its biblical force.

Of course, this doctrine does have important implications for the issue of church power (or, as the confession puts it in chap. 20, "liberty of conscience"). Our Puritan fathers were certainly right to argue that the regulative principle limits what the church authorities may "impose" on worshipers. The church may impose only what God commands for his worship—and, of course, whatever else is necessary in order for us to apply those commands with unity and order.[10]

Conclusion

On this understanding, the regulative principle limits what we may do in worship, but it also allows different sorts of applications, and therefore a significant area of liberty. Different churches legitimately apply God's commands in different ways. God commands us to sing; some churches may apply that command by singing three hymns in their services, others four. Some may sing primarily traditional hymns, others contemporary songs. God commands us to pray. Some churches may have one prayer, led by the minister, or many, led by members of the congregation. As we shall see more clearly in subsequent chapters, there is quite a large role in worship for human judgment, for human creativity, operating within the limits of God's word.

Certainly, the regulative principle should not be used, as some have used it, to enforce traditionalism in worship. Both in Scripture and in church history, the regulative principle has been a powerful weapon *against* the imposition of human traditions in the worship of God. Consider again the protests of Isaiah (Isa. 29:13) and Jesus (Matt. 15:8–9) against those who placed human traditions on the same level as Scripture. Also consider again the protest of the Puritans against those who claimed the right to impose ceremonies without scriptural warrant.[11]

Certainly, the regulative principle is a charter of freedom, not a burdensome bondage. The regulative principle sets us free from human traditions, to worship God his way. It limits our choices in the way a fish is limited to its watery habitat. When we break out of those limits, we discover death awaiting us, not freedom. To deny the regulative principle is to rebel against our loving Creator and then, paradoxically, to find ourselves in miserable bondage to human dogmatism.

In the remainder of this book, therefore, I will not urge anyone to conform to the Puritan style of worship or to any other style. In that respect, this book will be rather unusual, compared to most other worship books! Rather, I shall present the regulative principle as one that sets us free, within limits, to worship God in the language of our own time, to seek those applications of God's commandments which most edify worshipers in our contemporary cultures.[12] We must be both more conservative and more liberal than most students of Christian worship: conservative in holding exclusively to God's commands in Scripture as our rule of worship, and liberal in defending the liberty of those who apply those commandments in legitimate, though nontraditional, ways.

Questions for Discussion

1. Define the following terms: *regulative principle, circumstance, application, church power, traditionalism.*
2. Have you ever heard of the regulative principle before? Why do you think this principle is so little known today, considering its importance in Scripture and in the Protestant Reformation?
3. Does the worship of your church conform to the regulative principle? Look through a recent order of worship in your church. How many worship activities are applications of biblical commands? Which ones are not, if any?
4. What sorts of actions in worship services violate the regulative principle? Processions? Incense? Vestments? The sprinkling of holy water? Liturgical dance? Celebration of saints' days? Greeting those around you? Announcements? Are some of these things commanded by Scripture? Are some of them justifiable as applications of biblical commands?

5. Does the concept of "application" narrow the historic differences between Presbyterian and Lutheran-Episcopalian views of worship? Does it open a doorway to greater agreement?
6. How is the regulative principle related to the question of church power? Why is it dangerous to limit the regulative principle to that matter?
7. How do some people use the regulative principle to enforce traditional styles of worship? What is wrong with that? How does the regulative principle, as construed in this chapter, actually encourage freedom from tradition?

Notes

[1] I am assuming in this book the historic Christian doctrine of Scripture, which teaches that Scripture is the very word of God, the ultimate authority for Christian doctrine and life, infallible and inerrant. Those who have problems with this doctrine are urged to consult such works as B. B. Warfield, *The Inspiration and Authority of the Bible* (Philadelphia: Presbyterian and Reformed, 1967); E. J. Young, *Thy Word Is Truth* (Grand Rapids: Eerdmans, 1957); Meredith G. Kline, *The Structure of Biblical Authority* (Grand Rapids: Eerdmans, 1972).

[2] Some readers will note that although I earlier cited a list of passages such as Lev. 10:1–3 to show God's displeasure with illegitimate worship, I have not used this list to prove the regulative principle, but have instead relied on more general considerations. It does not seem to me that that list of passages proves the precise point that "whatever is not commanded is forbidden." The practices condemned in those passages are not merely not commanded; they are explicitly forbidden. For example, what Nadab and Abihu did in Lev. 10:1 was not only "unauthorized," the text informs us, but also "contrary to [God's] command." The fire should have been taken from God's altar (Num. 16:46), not from a private source (compare Ex. 35:3).

[3] Of course, it is "common to human actions and societies" for people to determine specific applications of general rules. Perhaps, then, we can, after all, speak of the choice of specific prayers as a "circumstance." But this is a fairly abstract logical point, and I doubt that the divines had it in mind when they mentioned "circumstances."

[4] It might be helpful for readers to compare this concept with the

discussion of "application" in my *Doctrine of the Knowledge of God*
(Phillipsburg, N.J.: Presbyterian and Reformed, 1987).

[5]I do subscribe to the confession's teaching at this point; I wish
only to supplement it. I agree with the confession that we must use our
own prudence in areas "common to human actions and societies." But
I believe that we must use our prudence in other areas as well. And although the confession does not mention matters such as the prayer example, I cannot believe that the divines were unaware of them. Certainly, to affirm the exercise of human prudence in such areas does not
contradict anything in the Westminster standards.

[6]Note that I qualify this statement with "normally" and "generally."
There is some overlap between the purposes of worship and those of
entertainment. For example, worship music often has aesthetic value;
the reading of God's word, when done well, has dramatic aspects; there
is humor in Scripture and in good preaching, as we shall see later. But
the purpose of these activities is not merely aesthetics, or drama, or
amusement; and we must beware lest these entertaining aspects of our
meetings overshadow our work of honoring God and edifying his people.

[7]The confession itself may teach such a comprehensive view of
scriptural sufficiency in 1.6. I am not sure that 1.6 is entirely consistent
with 20.2.

[8]Scripture does say, "Obey your leaders and submit to their authority" (Heb. 13:17). Do such leaders add to the commands of Scripture? No, for leaders in the church are themselves under the word of
God. As we shall see more fully in the next section, they may not presume to require anything of us beyond what Scripture requires.

[9]This example is something of an exaggeration, but it may be the
case that some in Israel did something very similar: they worshiped the
true God in the temple, and then worshiped contrary to God's commands in the "high places" (e.g., 1 Kings 3:3; 11:7–8).

Many Christians who claim to adhere strictly to the regulative
principle display this sort of inconsistency. I have worshiped in several
churches that conscientiously believe that a woman should never have
a leadership role in worship, but which permit a woman to lead a "song
service" ten minutes before the evening service. Why? Because, I am
told, the song service is not "official" worship, and therefore not subject to the regulative principle.

Similarly, there is a college that belongs to a denomination known
for taking the regulative principle very strictly. The denomination for-

bids the singing of hymns other than Psalm versions in worship services, and also forbids any instrumental accompaniment to congregational singing. Their college choir, however, sings hymns that are not based on the Psalms, and does so to instrumental accompaniment.

[10]This is true in all areas of life, not only worship in the narrow sense. The church may only require its members to obey the commands of Scripture, but that principle includes, rather than excludes, legitimate applications of those commands. For example, the church may proclaim, "Thou shalt not kill," a command of Scripture. But it may also proclaim, "Thou shalt not commit parricide, fratricide, genocide, or abortion," since those are legitimate applications of the biblical command, even though they are not explicitly mentioned in the Bible. If the preaching and discipline of the church are limited only to the explicit teachings of Scripture, then God's ministers may only read the Bible, not preach it—for preaching is application by its very nature.

[11]Do not misunderstand me here. I do not believe that every action we perform in church must be justified by a biblical proof text. It may be that some of the "ceremonies" against which the Puritans complained can be justified as applications of biblical commands. But the opponents of the Puritans believed that they had authority to command such ceremonies independently of the biblical commands, and the Puritans were right to deny that the church had such authority.

[12]Recall 1 Cor. 14:26, in which "the strengthening of the church" is the apostle's rule governing worship. You might also review our discussion in chap. 1 of the importance of both vertical and horizontal perspectives in worship.

5

What to Do in Worship

For the rest of the book, I intend to focus on the public worship of the church, setting aside for now other kinds of worship, such as private, family, civic, and "informal" worship (Sunday school, hymn sings, and the like), and worship in the "broad sense." These are all important; indeed, they deserve much more theological attention than they have received to date. But that study will have to await other occasions and perhaps other authors.

In this chapter I will seek to describe those events which are appropriate in the public worship of the church, in accordance with the regulative principle as I explained it in chapter 4. As I have indicated, God's basic method for regulating the public worship of the church is no different from his method of regulating other forms of worship, including worship in the broad sense. But I wish to focus now specifically on what God says in Scripture about public worship under the New Covenant in Christ.

The "Elements" of Worship

How should we use the regulative principle to generate a list of appropriate events for worship? The regulative principle requires us to worship according to God's commands. But what commands of Scripture are relevant to our question?

We might focus on the broadest, most general commands of Scripture, such as "Do it all for the glory of God" (1 Cor. 10:31) and "All of these must be done for the strengthening of the church" (1 Cor. 14:26), and seek to develop the structure of worship out of them. On that basis, we would simply ask, What brings glory to God? and, What brings strengthening (edification) to the church? We could then include in worship anything that seemed to us to be glorifying to God or edifying to the church. We could assure ourselves that our decisions were in accord with the regulative principle because we made them by applying the scriptural commands.

But that procedure seems to leave too much of the decision up to us. One of the main attractions of the regulative principle is that it forces us to seek God's direction for worship. But if, in the end, God only reveals the broadest generalities, then the whole discussion of the regulative principle hardly seems worth the effort.

Therefore, we, like our Puritan fathers, must wrestle with the problem of generality and specificity. If a particular practice accords with the regulative principle, surely, it must follow a more specific scriptural command than, say, 1 Corinthians 14:26. But how specific must it be? Do we need, for example, to find a specific command in the Bible to sing verse four of hymn 337? Surely not. But where is the happy medium? How specific are the commands that we are looking for?

In response to this kind of question, the Puritans developed the doctrine of "elements" or "parts" of worship. Worship, they believed, is made up of certain clearly distinguishable elements: prayer, the reading of Scripture, preaching, and so on. The regulative principle, they held, requires us to find biblical warrant for each of these elements. For them, that answered the question about the level of specificity. We need not find a biblical command to pray this or that particular prayer (assuming that the prayers under consideration are all scriptural in their content and appropriate to the occasion), but we do need a biblical warrant to include prayer as an element of worship.

But there are serious problems with this approach. The most serious problem is that there is no scriptural warrant for it! Scripture nowhere divides worship up into a series of independent "elements," each requiring independent scriptural justification. Scripture nowhere tells us that the regulative principle demands that particular level of specificity, rather than some other.

Further, this method of regulating worship runs into many practical snags. There have been many disagreements through the years over which practices in worship are actually elements and which are not. Some have claimed that the use of instruments to accompany singing is a possible element of worship, requiring specific scriptural authorization; others have said that the use of instruments is a mere circumstance (see our discussion of circumstances in chap. 4).[1] Some have said that singing is an element of worship; others have argued that it is merely a way of carrying out other elements (praise, teaching, confession, etc.). Even the English Puritans and the Scottish Presbyterians were divided on many of these questions, such as the propriety of reading written prayers, saying the Lord's Prayer, singing the *Gloria Patri*, reciting the Apostles' Creed, and having funeral and marriage services.[2] The issue at stake in these controversies was the issue of elements: which of these activities are elemental in character, demanding specific scriptural justification, and which may be justified as applications of other elements?

Do we need, for example, a specific biblical command to have marriage services? Or can marriage services be justified by the consideration that vows are a biblical element of worship and that the marriage service is essentially the taking of public vows? On the first interpretation, the regulative principle excludes marriage services; on the second, it permits them. How can we resolve such a question?

The problem is that Scripture doesn't give us a list of elements required for Christian worship services. In the Old Testament, God gave Israel an elaborate set of instructions for the construction of the tabernacle and the temple, and he stated in detail the requirements for the priesthood, the offerings, and the feasts. But he gave no specific directions at all for the worship of the synagogue. Indeed, the synagogue is hardly mentioned in the Old Testament, if at all; we know that God approved of it mainly from Jesus' attendance and teaching there.

The New Testament tells us a little more about the Christian meeting (which was more like the synagogue than like the sacrificial worship of the temple), but it gives us no systematic or exhaustive list of the events that were authorized for such services. Certainly it gives us no list of elements in the technical sense of Puritan theology—actions requiring specific scriptural authorization, as opposed to circumstances or applications that do not.

Another problem with the concept of elements of worship is that the things we do in worship are not always clearly distinguishable from one another. Singing and teaching, for example, are not distinct from one another. When we sing hymns with biblical content, we teach one another (Col. 3:16). And many hymns are also prayers and creeds. Prayers with biblical content contain teaching. The entire service is prayer, since it is uttered in the presence of God, to his praise. The entire service is teaching, since it is all based on Scripture. Perhaps it would be better to speak of "aspects" of worship, rather than "elements" or "parts."[3]

Making a List

So where does this discussion leave us? We need divine direction for worship: something more specific than 1 Corinthians 10:31 and 14:26. But the elaborate Puritan methodology for resolving these questions lacks coherence and biblical support. Where do we go from here?

The answer is not terribly hard to find. It is simply to obey everything that God says in Scripture about worship—to follow the whole counsel of God (Acts 20:27; compare Matt. 4:4).

God reveals to us general principles, such as 1 Corinthians 10:31. But he also reveals many relatively specific principles, such as James 2:1–4, where we are told not to discriminate in worship against people with poor clothing. Where specifics are lacking, we must apply the generalities by means of our sanctified wisdom, within the general principles of the word. Where specifics are given, we must accept them and apply them even more specifically to our own particular situations.

We must simply search the Scriptures to determine what is appropriate and inappropriate to do when the church meets together as a body in the name of the Lord Jesus. The Old Testament, as I indicated, nowhere lists the elements prescribed specifically for the meetings of the synagogue. Nevertheless, it is plain in the Old Testament that God is pleased when people gather for "sacred assembly," and that he approves of corporate prayer and the teaching of his word as ways of relating to his presence among them. Similarly, the New Testament does not give us an exhaustive list of what was and was not done at early Christian meetings. However, as in the case of the Old Testament synagogue, we may, by appeal to broad theological principles, gain assurance as to what God wants us to do when we gather in his name.

For example, there is no New Testament command to administer baptism in a Sunday meeting, and there is no historical record of that ever being done in the New Testament period. Baptisms in the New Testament are typically performed outside of formal meetings. But the nature of baptism, as a sign and seal of the covenant of grace, and as a solemn, public oath to the Lord and profession of faith in him, surely makes it appropriate as a part of public Christian worship. First, baptism cannot be other than public. Second, it is administered in the name of Christ, even *into* the name of Christ, and therefore is appropriately performed in a meeting held in Jesus' name. Third, it is the rite of entrance into the church; therefore, it must be witnessed by a gathering of at least some of the leadership of the church.

My List

Using this sort of reasoning, we can develop the following list of things to do in worship. I shall include, when necessary, some remarks as to why I believe these suggestions are scriptural.

1. *Greetings and Benedictions.* There is no specific biblical command to include these in public worship, nor is there any historical example during the New Testament period of them being uttered at the introduction or conclusion to public worship. Nevertheless, they were clearly part of church life, since they were a regular part of Paul's letters (see Rom. 1:7; 1 Cor. 1:3; Rom. 15:33; 1 Cor. 16:23–24; 2 Cor. 13:14). Since his letters were most likely read in church meetings (Col. 4:16; 1 Thess. 5:27; Philem. 2), these greetings and benedictions were also part of public worship. In these blessings, as in the great Aaronic benediction of Numbers 6:24–27, God identifies the congregation as his people, whom he wishes to bless with his grace and peace. The message of the blessing is part of God's word and therefore appropriate to public worship.

2. *Reading of Scripture.* In the synagogue, Scripture was read regularly (Luke 4:17–19; Acts 15:21; compare Deut. 31:9–13; Neh. 8). We know that there was also public reading of Scripture in the New Testament church (1 Tim. 4:13). Old Testament texts, which were crucial to the life of the church, may well have been read (see 2 Tim. 3:15–17). Eventually, Paul's letters were also read, as we saw in the previous paragraph. His letters were the rule in all the churches; therefore, they had to be made known to the people as God's word to them (2 Thess. 3:14; 1 Cor. 14:37; 2 Peter 3:15). Indeed, as we shall see, when God's word is read, God is personally present to his readers and hearers. So a public reading of God's word always creates a divine-human confrontation—an event of public worship.

3. *Preaching and Teaching.* God intended for his word to be taught, as well as read, in the assembly of the people (see Neh. 8:8; Luke 4:20; Acts 20:7; 1 Tim. 4:6; 5:17; 6:2; 2 Tim. 2:2; 3:16; 4:2; Titus 1:9). Preaching and teaching (which are not sharply distinguished in the New Testament) were part of the synagogue service and also part of the Christian meeting. The texts I have cited do not specify that teaching should take place in one particular official service, and certainly teaching took place in a

wide variety of situations (see Acts 2:1–14; 13:5; 20:20; etc.). But teaching is a public activity, and, as a communication between God and his people, it creates a situation of worship whenever and wherever it is done. Surely it is appropriate to any situation in which God's people meet to worship him.

4. *Charismatic Prophecy and Speaking in Tongues.* Earlier I indicated my belief that these were special gifts of God for the founding of the church and should not be expected in our time. Nevertheless, it is plain that these were part of the Christian meeting in the New Testament period (1 Cor. 14).

5. *Prayer.* No argument is needed to indicate that corporate prayer is a legitimate part of public worship (see Acts 2:42; 1 Cor. 14:16; 1 Tim. 2:1–2). In Scripture, there are many types of prayer, including praise, petition, lament, confession of sin, expressions of repentance, and thanksgiving.

6. *Song.* God clearly wants his people to sing when meeting together in his name (see 1 Chron. 16:9; 1 Cor. 14:26; Eph. 5:19–20; Col. 3:16). However, I do not believe that song is an element of worship as elements are defined within the Puritan system. Song does not have an independent function in worship; rather, it is a way of doing many different things: praying, teaching, blessing, fellowshiping, etc.

7. *Vows.* In making a vow, we solemnly call upon God to witness our statements and promises. In Scripture, this is typically a public act, involving other people as witnesses. Therefore, Scripture typically associates it with public worship (Pss. 22:25; 50:14; 65:1; 76:11; compare the Westminster Confession of Faith, 22.1). Vows are involved in baptism, the Lord's Supper (as the renewal of God's covenant with us), the reception of new church members, the ordination of church officers, marriage, and indeed, more broadly, the consecration of our lives to God's purposes. All public worship includes the congregation's vow to serve Christ as Lord.

8. *Confession of Faith.* In confession, we profess our faith before men. All public worship is confession, for as we go to church, we tell the world that we are servants of Jesus. Confession results in salvation (Matt. 10:32; Luke 12:8; Rom. 10:9–10), and it distinguishes between the people of God and those of the world (1 John 4:2–3, 15). Scripture often refers to confession in a context of public worship (1 Kings 8:33–35; 2 Chron. 6:24–26; 30:22; Heb. 13:15). Paul speaks of Timothy's "good confession in the presence of many witnesses," reflecting Jesus' own "good confession" before Pilate (1 Tim. 6:12–13). It is therefore entirely appropriate that God's people recite creeds in public worship to confess their faith as a body of believers.

9. *Sacraments.* In regard to baptism, see the discussion earlier in this chapter. The New Testament Christians clearly observed the Lord's Supper together (1 Cor. 11:17–34). Paul's descriptions of the sacrament as the new covenant in Jesus' blood (11:25), a proclamation of the Lord's death (v. 26), and "a participation" in the body and blood of Christ (10:16) make it plain that the Supper is a part of public worship.

10. *Church Discipline.* In Matthew 18:15–20, Jesus teaches his disciples how to deal with sin in the church. They are not to ignore it; rather, they are to confront the sinner. First, the aggrieved party is to go to him privately. If that does not resolve the issue, he is to try again, accompanied by witnesses. If the second confrontation fails, the matter should be taken "to the church," and may result in excommunication. Although modern churches are rather ignorant of their responsibilities in this regard, Jesus promises his special presence with the church that carries out this responsibility (v. 20). The reference to Jesus' special presence suggests that the Lord regards discipline as an act of worship. The apostle Paul in 1 Corinthians 5:4–5 makes it clear that some judgments are to be pronounced in the assembly.

11. *Collections, Offerings.* In the Old Testament, the term "offering" usually refers to sacrifices brought to the tabernacle

or the temple. In New Testament worship, we do not bring offerings of that sort to God, since Jesus has given his life as the once-for-all sacrifice. But we do bring ourselves to God as living sacrifices. And there are opportunities to bring gifts for God's purposes and for the relief of the poor (see Gal. 2:10; 1 Cor. 9:3–12). In 1 Corinthians 16:1–2, Paul tells the church to collect gifts on the first day of the week, the day of the church meeting. On another occasion, he indicates that the giving of gifts is an act of worship: "[The gifts] are a fragrant offering, an acceptable sacrifice, pleasing to God" (Phil. 4:18). Thus, many churches refer to the collection as an "offering," even though that term may cause some confusion with the sacrifices of the Old Testament. In any case, I conclude that the collection, by whatever name, is properly worship—something the church should do when assembled in God's name.

12. *Expressions of Fellowship.* In chapter 1, I indicated that worship has both vertical and horizontal aspects—that in worship we should be concerned above all for God's glory, but also for our fellow worshipers as our brothers and sisters in Christ. That horizontal focus can be seen in our prayers for one another, in our exhorting of one another through preaching and teaching (Heb. 10:24–25), in the greetings and benedictions, in confessions and vows, in church discipline, in the sacraments (see 1 Cor. 10:14–17; 11:17–34), and in the collection of gifts. There are other ways, too, in which the New Testament Christians showed their love for one another and their unity in Christ:

a. One was the "love feast" (*agape*), a fellowship meal held in conjunction with the Lord's Supper. Only Jude 12 (and possibly 2 Peter 2:13, on one reading) refers to the love feast directly, but there are many references to it after the New Testament period, and Paul clearly describes it in 1 Corinthians 11:20–22, 33–34 (see also Acts 2:42–47; 4:35; 6:1; 20:7–11). Because of the abuses noted in 1 Corinthians, the *agape* was eventually separated from the Lord's Supper, and still later was abandoned entirely. Yet it raises the possibility, even for us today, that a fellowship meal could be considered part of worship. Surely it was a public event, a meeting of the church, and the love in view was the love of Jesus.

b. Another expression of Christian love was the "holy kiss" (Rom. 16:16; 1 Cor. 16:20; 2 Cor. 13:12; 1 Thess. 5:26; 1 Peter 5:14). Holy kisses were perhaps exchanged during worship, just as people shake hands and greet one another in many churches today. Is this worship? Well, the kiss is not an ordinary kiss, but a "holy" one. I understand this to mean that the greeting, in God's presence, sets apart the worshipers as members of the body of Christ, declaring their love for one another in Jesus. We should remember that love is, in a very important sense, a "mark of the church"—that which distinguishes the church from the world (John 13:34–35).

Therefore, it is appropriate for us to say and do things in worship to encourage our friendship for one another in the Lord. For example, some people think that announcements during the service are a distraction from worship. I agree that announcements can often be an annoyance, because of their length, frequency, or inappropriate presentation. However, I believe that it is appropriate in worship to announce opportunities for further teaching, ministry, and general "body life" (including social events).

And I believe it is entirely proper in worship to give public thanks to people in the congregation (and to God for them) who have in some special way served God and their brothers and sisters in Christ. Notice how Paul does this in Philippians 1:3–6; 4:10–19—a letter that was doubtless read during worship to the church at Philippi. It is not wrong in worship to honor human beings, as long as that honor does not compromise the supreme honor due to the Lord. Nor is it wrong for the congregation to express that honor with a song, applause, hand holding, or hugs. These actions are the languages of Christian love.

Concluding Observations

So far, my list of "things to do in worship" has been a very general one. There are many specific actions that are also mentioned in Scripture, such as clapping hands (Pss. 47:1; 97:8), raising hands (Pss. 63:4; 134:2; 1 Tim. 2:8), choir singing and instrumental music (Ex. 15; 1 Chron. 25:1–31; Ps. 150), congregational responses (Deut. 27:15; Pss. 118:2–4; 136; 1 Cor. 14:16), dance (Ex. 15:20; Jer. 31:4, Pss. 149:3; 150:4), and choosing leaders (Acts 1:12–26). I shall discuss some of these more specific matters elsewhere in the book. I shall also discuss various proposals for worship that arise out of the need to apply the above list. For example, some churches use drama as a way of preaching or teaching the word. I shall later discuss whether this is legitimate.

I do not believe that the list of worship events should be used in a mechanical way. For example, some might suppose that every item in the list must be found in every worship service. In my view, that view goes beyond Scripture. Nor should we assume that every meeting of the church must be limited to the items on that list. Not every meeting of the church must be devoted exclusively to worship in the narrow sense.

Still, the list provides us with some general guidance. The various items are things that God wants us to do when we meet in his name. We should therefore avoid activities that crowd them out or compromise their integrity. When Paul tells the Corinthians to satisfy their hunger at home rather than during the assembly (1 Cor. 11:22), he is not saying that a fellowship meal is inappropriate in a worship context; indeed, his discussion presupposes the legitimacy of the love feast. What he is forbidding is conduct that compromises the meaning and purpose of the Lord's Supper. That is, in my opinion, the key to what we must exclude from worship. Scripture gives us no definitive list of "elements" that alone must be present in the "official" service. But it does tell us to avoid practices and attitudes that compromise the scripturally defined purposes of the meeting.

Questions for Discussion

1. First Corinthians 14:26 tells us in worship to do all things "for the strengthening of the church." Does this verse tell us everything we need to know about worship, or does God

want to tell us something more? How does the Puritan doctrine of elements deal with this question?

2. How does the synagogue create a problem for the concept
   of divinely ordained elements of worship? Does Scripture
   provide a list of elements for New Testament worship? For
   New Testament "official" worship?

3. Is it possible to establish the legitimacy of some activity in
   worship when there is no explicit scriptural command or example? Consider baptism as an example.

4. Is there anything you would add to my list? Is there anything
   you would remove from it? Why?

5. What is church discipline? Why is it an act of worship?

6. Should we have love feasts in the church today? Should we
   serve the Lord's Supper at potluck suppers? Are potluck suppers, then, in effect, worship services? Discuss.

7. Should we kiss each other during worship? Shake hands?
   Hug? All of the above? None? Argue your position.

Notes

[1]Churches in the Covenanter tradition, such as the Reformed
Presbyterian Church of North America, often justify the use of pitch
pipes as "circumstances," while rejecting the use of organs and pianos
as unauthorized "elements." The logic of this distinction escapes me.
If it is legitimate to use a pitch pipe to give the congregation the first
note of a song, why shouldn't we also give the congregation help with
the second note, the third, the harmony, and the rhythm?

[2]See R. J. Gore, review of *Worship in the Presence of God,* ed. by Frank
Smith and David Lachman, in *Westminster Theological Journal* 56 (Fall
1994): 445.

[3]Readers of my previous books will understand when I say that the
term "perspective" also occurs to me in this context.

6

Arrangements for Worship

In the previous chapter, we asked what we should do in worship. In this chapter, we will consider the when and where of worship. We shall also consider the matter of leadership, since it is important to know who is responsible for ordering worship according to the word of God. In general, we shall be asking how we can apply an important scriptural principle, namely, the command to do all things "in a fitting and orderly way" (1 Cor. 14:40).

Leadership

The Lord Jesus Christ rules his church through his *apostles*. The apostles have left their teaching to us in the writings of the New Testament, in which they also testify to the authority of the Old Testament in the church (2 Tim. 3:16–17; 2 Peter 1:19–21). The *elders* teach the word of God and administer the affairs of the church according to the word (Acts 14:23; 15:2; 1 Tim. 5:1, 17; Titus 1:5). Elders are sometimes called *bishops* or overseers (Phil. 1:1; 1 Tim. 3:2). Elders are assisted by *deacons* (Phil. 1:1; 1 Tim. 3:8–13; Acts 6:1–7;[1] Rom. 16:1[!]). We may assume, then, that since the apostles are dead, the worship of the church is under the control of the elders. It is their responsibility to make sure that the worship of the church is acceptable to God according to Scripture.

From this premise, some have argued that only an ordained elder may preside at a worship service (or an "official"[2] worship service).[3] They argue that Scripture mentions nobody else as qualified to lead in worship. But that argument is weak. One might as easily argue that since the elders have the overall responsibility for teaching in the church, only an ordained elder may teach three-year-olds.

Part of the problem is that there is an ambiguity in the term *leadership* in this sort of context. It may mean overall "control," or it may mean "presiding at an assembly." Clearly, in the first sense the elders are the "leaders," according to Scripture. But Scripture is silent as to who may or may not preside at church meetings. Because of that silence, the elders have freedom to preside at church meetings or to appoint others to do it under their authority.[4]

Although Scripture does not tell us specifically who may or may not preside, it is plain that during New Testament worship services many voices were heard: "When you come together, everyone has a hymn, or a word of instruction, a revelation, a tongue or an interpretation" (1 Cor. 14:26). To be sure, many of these speakers uttered prophecies and tongues of a sort that God no longer gives to the church. But the overall structure of the meeting seems rather democratic—of course, under the general oversight of the eldership. It is certainly far from the model of many present-day churches, in which only the minister speaks extemporaneously, and the congregation is silent except when singing or speaking together from a hymnal or other predetermined script. In the worship described in 1 Corinthians 14, many people suggested things to do in worship. Obviously, someone appointed by the elders had to be in charge of keeping order; Paul urges greater attention to that in verse 40 and throughout the chapter. But he doesn't mention any such leader or leaders;

he places the responsibility of keeping order upon the whole congregation.[5]

It is also important in such discussions to remember the nature of leadership in the church. Jesus teaches that leadership is not to be authoritarian; rather, the leaders should *serve* those under their authority, as Jesus gave his life for his people (Matt. 20:25–28; compare 1 Peter 5:3). Further, since all believers are priests (1 Peter 2:9), it is not the job of the elders to do all the work of the church, but rather, as servant-leaders, to help the congregation exercise their gifts (Rom. 12:1–8; 1 Cor. 12:1–31) to build up the body of Christ. This teaching also suggests that in worship many voices should be heard, that many suggestions should be honored, and that competence to preside at worship may be found broadly throughout the church.[6]

This is not to minimize the importance of elder oversight or of the special gifts necessary for a worship leader. Although it may well be that one can have the ability to lead worship without having the gifts requisite for the eldership, nevertheless the leadership of worship is a spiritual responsibility. It should be given only to those who are mature in their faith, who understand the biblical view of worship, and who can in their words and actions model the truth and the love of Christ. The leader must also be sensitive to how his demeanor affects the atmosphere and content of worship.

And certainly it is also important that the elders, whether or not they are presiding over the meeting, oversee the various suggestions made by the people, to make sure that those suggestions are in accord with the word of God.

Occasions for Worship

Worship is appropriate at any time. However, as we saw in our discussion of Old Testament worship, God ordained the Sabbath day as a holy day, set apart to himself out of all the other days of the week. On that day he commanded Israel to gather for "sacred assemblies." Therefore, the Sabbath was especially appropriate as an occasion for worship. Together with the divinely appointed feast days, it was the time for Israel's regular worship.

I do not have space here to defend adequately my view of the Sabbath in the New Covenant. With the Reformed tradition, I believe that the fourth commandment of the Decalogue is still binding, although the system of feasts and sabbatical years is abrogated in the New Testament. Christians observe the Sabbath on the first day of the week rather than the seventh, celebrating Jesus' resurrection. Jesus' words concerning the Sabbath, for example in Mark 2:27–28, do not hint at an abrogation of the Sabbath, but rather indicate that the Sabbath continues under his lordship. And "the Lord's Day" of Revelation 1:10 seems to me to be a clear exception to the general New Testament principle that every day is like every other one (Rom. 14:5).[7] First Corinthians 16:1–2 indicates that the early church met on the first day of the week.

On this view, as the Puritans insisted, there is only one "holy day" for Christians. But were they correct to forbid the celebration of Christmas and other "holidays"? Certainly they were right to distinguish between the Sabbath and all other days of the week. But does the celebration of Christmas (assuming it falls on a day other than Sunday) necessarily compete with the Sabbath day?

That depends, of course, on what we mean by "celebrate." Certainly God does not forbid people to work on Christmas, or require churches to have worship services on Christmas or Christmas Eve. We should not regard Christmas as we regard the Sabbath. But Christians who observe Christmas do not normally see it as a "holy day" in competition with the Sabbath. It is merely a time to remember the Incarnation. Is it wrong to hold special services to remember particular biblical themes? I think not. Is it wrong for our regular services in the week before December 25 to focus on the birth of Jesus and its meaning for the salvation of sinners? Surely not. At that time of year, should we not take advantage of people's interest in the baby Jesus, as a means of edifying Christians and evangelizing the lost? I believe these questions answer themselves.

2. Reenactment of Redemption

Some people have tried to develop a scriptural case for a certain order of worship. They have noted various kinds of order in Scripture: the architecture of the tabernacle, from altar to basin to bread of the Presence, lampstand, incense, and ark; the order of offerings (sin, consecration, fellowship) in Leviticus 9; the order of the worship in the book of Revelation. These passages have been thought to suggest a certain order of worship: the forgiveness of sin, consecration of the forgiven sinner through the ministry of the word, fellowship with God in the Lord's Supper. An order of worship so structured amounts to a reenactment of redemption. Jesus deals with our sin, consecrates our lives to him in covenant, and then fellowships with us through his Spirit. This reenactment reinforces the basic message of the gospel: Christ is our Savior from sin, the Lord whom we obey, the reconciled friend who calls us to table fellowship. Therefore, it has been the dominant pattern of liturgy throughout the history of the church.

But worship arranged around the same thematic structure week after week can easily lose its power to communicate the freshness of God's truth. And it is difficult within that structure (though, of course, not impossible) to find ways of emphasizing other biblical themes, such as the reality of God and his attributes, the deity and humanity of Christ, the Resurrection, the doctrines of calling, adoption, and sanctification, stewardship of possessions, sexual purity, and so on.

Furthermore, an important theological point is obscured by the reenactment liturgy. That is that redemption is in the past, accomplished once for all. The reenactment liturgy somewhat obscures the fact that we enter worship, not as lost sinners confronting a wrathful God, but as "saints" (Rom. 1:7; 1 Cor. 1:2, etc.) who have already made our peace with God through Christ. The great fact governing the worship experience from beginning to end is that Christ's work is complete, that he is raised from the dead. Doubtless there is a place in worship for asking God's forgiveness of our continuing sins for the sake of Christ. But wor-

The Order of Events

1. The Historical Approach

Theologians have argued much over the question of the order of worship: what should come before what? Sometimes that question has been answered historically, by reference to what we know of the practice of the synagogue and the practice of the church in the New Testament period and since then. Actually, however, we know very little of the church's liturgy in the first century. And although it is interesting to study the worship of the synagogue and of the later church, Christian believers are not bound by historical practices as such, but only by the word of God.[8]

Certainly we can learn valuable things from a study of the history of worship. Many have testified as to the value in present-day worship of historical practices that establish a solidarity between the present-day believer and believers of past ages. In one sense, we worship together with them (Heb. 12:23), and they are still our teachers. Certainly there is value in cultivating a sense of the body of Christ of all ages.

On the other hand, Scripture also tells us, and more explicitly and emphatically, that worship should be intelligible. It should be understandable to the worshipers, and even to non-Christian visitors (1 Cor. 14, especially vv. 24–25). And intelligibility requires contemporaneity. When churches use archaic language and follow practices that are little understood today, they compromise that biblical principle.

There is no reason why the church cannot attain both historicity and contemporaneity. Most of the historic practices of the church are quite intelligible today and can be stated in contemporary language. But we should avoid slavish imitation of older practices without attention to the matter of communication. To say this is merely to call us back to our fundamental task, which Jesus set forth in the Great Commission (Matt. 28:18–20)—the task of discipling, baptizing, and teaching all nations. That divine mandate, rather than any human traditions, must ultimately guide our decisions about the order of worship.

shipers should not be led to suppose (as in the Roman Catholic view of the Mass as a repeated sacrifice) that the work of redemption needs to be done over and over again. All churches need to take pains to counter that misunderstanding, but especially churches that lead worshipers week after week through the reading of the law, the confession of sins, and the assurance of pardon.

It seems to me to be more in line with the emphasis of the New Testament to have a service that stresses primarily the joy of the resurrection of Jesus. After all, we meet for worship on the first day of the week in order to commemorate that event. Of course, that joy must be defined as a joy in the accomplishment of the Atonement and of the fullness of the forgiveness of sins. And there must be a proper place in worship for confession of sin and assurance of forgiveness through the seal of Jesus' resurrection. I am proposing a difference in emphasis, rather than substance. But we should not simply assume that the reenactment liturgy, because of its historical prestige, has no disadvantages.

In the final analysis, the texts mentioned at the beginning of this section were never intended by God to provide a required order of worship for the New Testament church. Therefore, we are free to vary the thematic content of worship within biblical limits. This variation need not displace the basic gospel of forgiveness, consecration, and fellowship with God. Indeed, the other biblical themes cannot be fully expounded without that basic gospel being prominent.

3. Dialogue

Another way in which theologians have tried to argue for a normative order of worship is by means of the concept of "divine-human dialogue."[9] Some of the meetings in Scripture between God and man have a dialogue structure: God speaks, man responds, God speaks again, and so on (see, for example, Gen. 28; Isa. 6; Jer. 1; Rev. 1). Dialogical worship typically alternates between events in which God speaks and events in which the congregation responds. Often there are sentences pronounced by the minister, followed by responsive sentences by the congregation.[10]

Christian worship certainly contains elements both of God's speaking (the greeting and blessing, the reading and preaching of Scripture) and of the congregation's responding (prayer, praise, song). The dialogue structure reminds us that salvation is by grace, by God's initiative, and that our obedience is a response to that grace.

But Scripture does not teach that the Christian meeting must be structured as a dialogue. For one thing, many divine-human encounters in the Bible itself are not notably dialogical. Many prayers and psalms in Scripture occur without any divine speech immediately before or after. And there are long speeches of God in the Prophets and elsewhere with no evident human response. Job 1–37 consists mostly of monologues by Job and his friends; chapters 38–42 are mostly divine monologue, with Job replying briefly, mainly to admit his disqualification to enter the discussion (40:1–5; 42:1–6)—hardly what liturgists typically call "participatory."

Another problem with the dialogue model is that, in one sense, in worship God is always speaking and we are always responding. God speaks, not only in the reading and preaching of Scripture, but also in the hymns, for good hymns express biblical content and therefore teach the word of God (Col. 3:16). The same thing is true of prayers. Indeed, a good service of worship contains biblical content from beginning to end, and in all of that we hear God's voice. On the other hand, in all of worship the congregation responds. In a sermon, the preacher not only speaks for God, but also expresses his own response to God's word. Also during the sermon, the congregation should be responding by seeking new paths of obedience. Therefore, there is no neat division in worship between some events at which God speaks and others in which we respond.

There are other dangers in the concept of dialogical worship, too. (1) The horizontal dimension, in which believers build up one another, is neglected. We have noted the importance of this dimension in passages like Hebrews 10:24–25. It is not clear how believer-to-believer dialogue fits into the model of the divine-human dialogue. (2) The minister tends to adopt an authoritarian role, since he typically represents God in this sort of service. (3) The congregational role is reduced to scripted "responses," as opposed to the broad use of congregational gifts suggested in 1 Corinthians 14.

4. Conclusions

There is no passage or principle in Scripture that dictates one invariable order of events in worship. There are, however, logical relations among the various aspects of worship that should not be ignored as we plan our worship services. It is important to remember, however, that there is more than one logical sequence agreeable to Scripture. Writers on worship tend to fixate on one such sequence (such as dialogue or forgiveness-consecration-fellowship), ignoring other biblically sound ways of structuring worship. Why, for example, should we not begin a service in praise to the risen Christ, and then at a later point recall that he was raised for the sake of our justification, our forgiveness of sins? Psalm 100:4 tells us to "enter his gates with thanksgiving and his courts with praise." And the Lord's Prayer instructs us to hallow God's name even before it calls us to ask forgiveness for our sins. Of course, true praise, like the pleasing sacrifice of Psalm 51:19, flows from a broken and contrite heart, whether that contrition is expressed first or later in worship.[11]

Why should we not spend an extended time singing to encourage one another to bring the gospel to the unbelieving world, and then confess that we too were once dead in trespasses and sins? Why should we not begin with a sermon about God as the Creator of all things, then sing praises to his greatness and his love for his sinful creatures? Every biblical doctrine is involved in each of the others;[12] why should we not explore the biblical paths from one to another in many ways, in many orders, from many directions?

As another example, consider the doxology. Some writers are very confident that they know the place in worship where the doxology truly "belongs." But the doxology is an expression of praise to God that simultaneously calls all creatures in heaven and on earth to praise him. Surely there are many places in worship where the doxology is appropriate, not just one or two. Consider how the apostle Paul in his letters breaks off his arguments in the oddest places to insert doxologies—as in Romans 1:25 and 2 Corinthians 11:31.

A recovery of biblical flexibility here can bring a new freshness to our worship, and freshness increases intelligibility, the power of our communication of God's word. Of course, there is also value in constancy. If everything changes from week to week, communication may be hindered rather than helped. The balance between regularity and flexibility requires considerable spiritual wisdom.

The Setting of Worship

Scripture gives no command as to where New Testament believers may or may not worship. In the Old Testament, prayer and teaching could take place anywhere, but sacrifice was restricted to the central altar in the tabernacle and the temple. In the New Testament, Jesus removes that restriction, for he himself is our sacrifice, our priest, and our central altar. And he resides, not at some earthly location, but in heaven—and, by his Spirit, in and with his people, wherever they may be (see John 4:19–24). Consequently, Christians may worship equally well in homes, outdoors, or in public buildings.

Therefore, the setting of worship is a matter that we are free to order according to our own God-given wisdom, in accordance with the general rules of the Word.

One of the most important of those general rules is the prohibition of idols throughout Scripture, especially in the second of the Ten Commandments. God's people are not to make images (either of the true God or of other gods) for the purpose of bowing down to them.

This command does not exclude all pictures from the worship area. The tabernacle and the temple themselves contained, at God's direction, many pictures and images (see Ex. 25:17–22, 31–36; 26:1–6; 1 Kings 6:29; 2 Chron. 4:2–3). What the commandment forbids is paying homage to images as channels or mediators of the Deity.

Scripture does not, therefore, forbid the use of pictures, banners, or decorations in the area used for Christian worship. Of course, some caution is needed, lest worshipers gain a sentimental attachment to some picture, which degenerates into idolatry. It can happen.

However, I do not think there is any scriptural reason to prefer, as some Puritans did, a plain worship area. Scripture nowhere urges plainness as a matter of principle. Ornateness can, of course, be distracting; but, similarly, a plain setting can detract from the solemnity and wonder of the divine-human encounter.

What about symbols, such as crosses, fish signs, and so on? Some in the Presbyterian tradition have ruled these out on the ground that symbols must be based on explicit divine commands. Thus, they reject all visible symbols except the sacraments. However, I have earlier argued that the biblical regulative principle does not require a specific divine command for each detail of the Christian meeting. We do have the general command to communicate God's revelation, and there is no reason why that cannot be done through visible symbols as well as by the written and spoken word. And we have the precedent of Old Testament worship, which freely employed symbolism.

Furthermore, we cannot escape from symbolism without escaping from the world itself. We live in a "sacramental universe," for God has created the whole world as a means of revealing himself (Ps. 19:1; Rom. 1:19–20). Jesus' teaching freely employs illustrations from nature: plentiful harvest fields, the ripening of plants and weeds, and so on. If we worship out-of-doors, we are surrounded by symbols of God's truth. And when Israel worshiped indoors, the decorations and colors spoke eloquently of God's creation and redemption. We ourselves, as God's image, represent God. And human language is a symbolism. If we were to restrict the use of symbols in worship only to those explicitly authorized in Scripture, then we could use only the words in Scripture itself. Indeed, even the use of Bible translations would be debatable. Ironically, some Puritans who advocated a plain worship setting used that very plainness to symbolize the clarity of the gospel.

Questions for Discussion

1. What is the responsibility of elders for the worship of the church? What may they delegate to others? What may they not delegate?
2. What ambiguity in the term *leadership* has led some to think that only elders should preside at church meetings?
3. How does leadership in the church differ from leadership in the non-Christian world? How does this difference affect the nature of leadership in worship?
4. Is it important to maintain historic traditions in worship? If so, what other biblical principle must also come into play so as to maintain balance?
5. Explain several principles that have been proposed to determine the order of worship. Are any of them binding upon all churches? What are some of the disadvantages in following these principles?
6. What are the arguments for and against the use of visible symbols in the worship area? Do such symbols violate the second commandment? Why or why not?

Notes

[1]The seven men mentioned in Acts 6 are not called "deacons," and some interpreters believe that they were more equivalent to the elders of the later church. We should not assume that these offices were always rigidly defined. There may have been flexibility from time to time and from church to church in the structure of the leadership.

[2]Compare our discussion of the "official-unofficial" distinction in chap. 4. Again, I would emphasize that Scripture does not make this distinction in setting forth God's standards for worship.

[3]Those who maintain that only elders may preside over worship

usually make an exception for men preparing for the ordained ministry. But that exception shows that this view does not arise from an absolute scriptural principle.

[4]Compare Gerhard Delling's comment that "it by no means follows that leading functions in Worship were joined with those in the leadership of the Church" (*Worship in the New Testament* [Philadelphia: Westminster, 1962], 34n).

[5]In the synagogue, any Jewish man could read the Scripture. It is hard for me to believe that the New Testament church was more restrictive than that.

[6]There is, of course, an important question about the role of women in worship. In general, I agree with James Hurley, *Man and Woman in Biblical Perspective* (Grand Rapids: Zondervan, 1981), and others, who argue that the only biblical limitation on women's role is that women may not be elders. Hurley argues that the prohibition on women speaking in 1 Cor. 14:34–35 is not for the duration of the meeting, but for the authoritative "weighing of the prophets" described in vv. 29–33, and that the teaching prohibited in 1 Tim. 2:12 is the authoritative teaching of the office of elder. However we may interpret these difficult passages, it is plain that under some circumstances women did legitimately speak in worship (1 Cor. 11:5) and that women were not entirely excluded from teaching (Acts 18:26; Titus 2:4).

[7]For a fuller argument, see John Murray, *The Sabbath Institution* (London: Lord's Day Observance Society, 1953). It is republished in *Collected Writings of John Murray*, vol. 1 (Edinburgh: Banner of Truth, 1976), 205–18, along with other papers on the subject.

[8]Delling describes the synagogue liturgy and then comments (*Worship in the New Testament*, 43), "It is clear that no influence of this service on the structure of the primitive Christian service is demonstrable. The essential parts of the former are lacking in the latter, and *vice versa;* only isolated formulae are taken over (Chap. V). Certainly the Jewish-Christian section of the primitive Christians attended the synagogue service; but they built up independently their own celebrations as a whole in the Jewish-Christian and in the Gentile-Christian areas. That was necessary because of the entirely different content of their life and faith."

He says (p. 43n) that those who argue that there was a strong synagogue influence on primitive Christian worship are drawing inferences "from a later time" and reading them back into the New Testament. In his view, the synagogue influence came later: "When the need was felt for a kind of pattern, attention turned to the models of the Jewish world, and the attempt was made to Christianise them."

[9]The dialogue structure may, of course, be used within the context of the order discussed in the previous paragraph, or in the context of some other topical structure.

[10]Synagogue worship also had something of a dialogue structure. But see the comments of Delling in note 8 about the relation of the synagogue to early Christian worship.

[11]Thanks to Thom Notaro for these observations on the Lord's Prayer and Pss. 51 and 100.

[12]They are "perspectival," as I sometimes like to say. See my *Doctrine of the Knowledge of God* (Phillipsburg, N.J.: Presbyterian and Reformed, 1987).

7

The Tone of Worship

The Emotions

When we refer to the "tone" or "atmosphere" or "style" of worship, we are usually thinking about the overall impact of the service upon the emotions of the worshiper. But even to speak of emotions in this connection creates embarrassment for some. Literature on worship, especially in Reformed circles, is full of condemnations of "emotionalism," especially in the charismatic movement and some other forms of evangelicalism. But there is little in this literature on the positive value of emotions in worship or the emotional content of the word of God.

Reformed theology has always been rather uneasy about the emotions. It has sometimes advocated the "primacy of the intellect": the view that truth comes to a person first through the intellect and only subsequently is applied to the will and the emotions. In my view, this doctrine is unscriptural, an intrusion of Greek philosophy into Christian thought. Certainly, God made the intellect to inform our actions and feelings, and there are grave dangers in living by one's feelings apart from intellectual reflection.[1] But in Scripture, God addresses his word, not to "the

77

intellect," but to the whole person, to the "heart." It is the whole person who has fallen into sin and must be redeemed.

It is best to think of intellect, will, and emotions as interdependent. Each affects the others, and none can function properly apart from the others.[2] When we try to employ one without the others, the result is distorted understanding, choices, and feelings. The emotions provide the intellect with data for analysis and judgment; the intellect provides the emotions with direction and perspective.

Therefore, in the Scriptures God appeals to us in a wide variety of ways, some relatively intellectual (for example, the letter to the Romans) and some relatively emotional (for example, the Psalms), but neither exclusively so—consider the emotional appeals of Romans 8:31–39 and 11:33–36 and the intellectual logic of Psalm 1. The emotional content of Scripture is part of the revelation of God. The very excitement that Paul expresses in Romans 11:33–36 conveys to us something of the heart of God himself—a revelation of God that we would not have if Paul had limited himself to abstract prose. The use of Scripture in worship should convey all of that emotional content, not just bare information.

Scripture also has much to say about our own emotional life—how we should feel about things. It speaks of joy, peace, anxiety, fear, courage, and love—concepts that are partly emotional in character.

Reformed worship has, unfortunately, often followed too much the model of an academic lecture. Ulrich Zwingli in Zurich eliminated music entirely from the service, focusing almost exclusively on teaching.[3] Later Reformed leaders were less extreme, but the model of worship as a teaching meeting has had great influence, especially in Puritanism. It is important that people of Reformed conviction give more positive attention to the emotional component of worship.

How the Worshiper Should Feel

Not all of the following qualities are emotions pure and simple, but each describes an attitude that we should bring to worship.

1. *Reverence.* This is an attitude of profound respect toward another. Scripture says that we should worship God "with reverence and awe" (Heb. 12:28). Roughly synonymous with this concept is "the fear of God" (Pss. 2:11; 5:7, and frequently elsewhere), which in Scripture is not terror of judgment (see Ex. 20:20; Prov 14:26), but the attitude of a faithful believer.

2. *Joy.* Scripture often associates joy with worship (see Pss. 2:11; 98:4–6; John 8:56; Acts 2:46; Jude 24; Rev. 19:7). We rejoice in God's reality, his presence with us, and his mighty acts of creation and redemption. Joy and reverence may at first glance appear to be contradictory. Practically speaking, it is difficult to maintain a balance between them. When a church seeks to emphasize the joy of worship, almost inevitably someone criticizes it for lacking reverence, and vice versa. Churches emphasizing reverence and those emphasizing joy often differ greatly in atmosphere, as much as funerals differ from parties. In Scripture, however, the two qualities are not opposed. Consider the remarkable conjunction of the two in Psalm 2:11: "Serve the LORD with fear and rejoice with trembling." How can reverent fear and joy be so closely linked?

The experience of meeting the one true God is overwhelming, and the emotional aspect of it is almost beyond description. But consider this illustration: Many of us have had the experience of being utterly surprised by a wonderful event—perhaps a lavish gift, an incredible kindness, or a life-changing opportunity. Sometimes such experiences arouse an emotion bordering on awe. We are struck speechless; we are overwhelmed. We try to imagine, but fail to conceive, how we could return such a great favor. Now add to this illustration the thought that the donor is omnipotent, omniscient, and omnipresent, and that he is the infinite, eternal, and unchangeable ruler of all creation, and you begin to understand something of the concept of biblical awe, which is at the same time joy raised to the highest degree. The title of C. S. Lewis's *Surprised by Joy,* with the explanation of the phrase in Lewis's text, perhaps points somewhat in the direction of what I am trying to describe.

Joyful worship in Scripture can be loud and energetic. It can be expressed in shouts and clapping (Pss. 47:1; 100:1; Zeph. 3:17).

3. *Sorrow for Sin.* Although sorrow for sin is certainly a legitimate aspect of worship, it should be understood as only a moment in worship, not a pervasive tone or atmosphere. In Psalm 51 and Isaiah 6, sorrow for sin soon dissolves into joy as the sinner finds forgiveness through the grace of God. There are, to be sure, some psalms where the mood of sorrow is unrelieved, but those psalms should be read in the overall context of Scripture, particularly in the light of Jesus' resurrection. The same should be said about lamentation over divine judgment and godly anger over injustice in the world (as in Pss. 73; 109; Lam. 1–5). These are legitimate moments in worship, but they should not set the overall tone (see Ps. 126:1–6). That overall tone should be one of reverent joy.

4. *Participation.* Worshipers should not take a passive attitude toward worship, such as we usually take toward entertainment. As we have seen, worship is a priestly service. It is *latreia,* "labor, service." Therefore, we should go to church to do something: to bring praise to God and to minister to one another. This perspective should make us less concerned about what we "get out of" worship and more concerned about what we contribute to God and to our brothers and sisters. It should encourage us to sing from the heart, to pray fervently, to hear God's word with the expectation that we will change our behavior in response, and to be a grateful guest at the Lord's Table. It should encourage us toward the relatively "democratic" structure of worship in 1 Corinthians 14, in which many people suggest things for the congregation to do, within a structure of decency and order.

Of course, as I emphasized earlier, there are blessings and benefits for each of us in worship. Indeed, worship is a celebration of God's *giving* and our *receiving.* That too motivates our participation. We participate with joy out of thanksgiving for God's wonderful grace.

Much has been said in recent worship literature about "participative" worship. In my view, some authors identify participation too narrowly with scripted congregational prayers and responses. Participation is something much more than that; it is a whole attitude toward the service. In my opinion, that attitude may well be lacking in churches that have elaborate patterns of responsive sentences, and it may be intense in churches that have a relatively simple pattern of singing, prayer, and sermon.

5. *Faith.* Faith is important to our entire relationship with God—and certainly to worship (Heb. 11:6; Rom. 14:23). Genuine faith generates an emotion of expectancy in worship: we trust God to keep his promises, to meet with us, to bless us in accordance with the gospel, to change our lives by the power of his word. A faithful worshiper will not go to church saying, "Oh, it's just going to be the same old thing again." And faithful worshipers will find their expectations fulfilled.

6. *Love.* Love for God and for one another embodies the whole of our responsibility before the Lord. It fulfills the law, because one who loves God will keep his law (Matt. 22:37–40; John 13:34–35; 14:15, 21). This is important both to the vertical and to the horizontal dimensions of worship.

7. *Boldness.* In the Old Testament period, only the high priest could enter the Most Holy Place in the tabernacle or the temple, and that only once a year, on the Day of Atonement, bringing blood to atone for his own sins and those of the people. When Jesus died, the veil separating the Most Holy Place from the Holy Place was torn in two from top to bottom. Thus, Jesus opened the way for all his people to enter into the presence of God as priests. We now have "boldness" to come into God's presence, in worship and particularly in prayer (Heb. 4:16; 10:19; 13:6; Eph. 3:12; compare 1 John 4:17).

We should be aware that this boldness marks a real difference between Old and New Testament worship. While reverence and awe are still important to the worship of God (Heb.

12:28), there is not as much distance separating us from God as there was in the Old Testament. We come before God as his mature sons and daughters. Our approach to God is not encumbered by scores of rules about sacrifices and blood offerings; those offerings have been completed in Christ. Whatever value there may be in ceremonies and in the circuitous approaches to the divine presence in the traditional liturgies, these are not necessary. Because of our union with Christ, we may simply and confidently walk into God's presence as his children, talk to him, and hear his words.

8. *Family Intimacy.* Jesus taught that in prayer we should address God as "Our Father." We are sons and daughters of God through Christ. As such, we love him and one another with an exclusive and rich love. To put it differently, we are not only servants (though we are that), but also friends (John 15:14–15). Remarkably, the New Testament nowhere commends formality in worship (or even "dignity," which is often a code word for formality). We simply gather as friends and family to commune with our Father and with Jesus (his Son and our older brother, Heb. 2:11–12).

Style and Atmosphere

Worship planners, as well as worshipers, need to give thought to the overall subjective tone of the worship service. For example, should it be formal or informal? Should it be quiet or noisy? Should the worship leader be friendly, chatty, humorous, or solemn in his demeanor? Should the congregation be absolutely quiet before the service to encourage meditation, or should they be encouraged to welcome visitors?

We can see that Scripture allows considerable freedom in these areas if we can cure ourselves of certain common prejudices. For example, it is sometimes thought that only formal worship in a solemn atmosphere can adequately encourage proper reverence and awe of the divine presence. But there is no scriptural reason to suppose that this is true. It is simply a human judgment that some may make and others may not. In this area, it is hard to get beyond anecdotal evidence. For what it is worth, I can remember any number of "informal" services in which I have been overwhelmed by the majesty of God. And it may be argued with equal plausibility that only informal, friendly worship does justice to the biblical motifs of the church as a family and our right of bold access to our heavenly Father.

Some may think that humor necessarily trivializes worship. But that is not true, for there is humor in Scripture, for example in Genesis 18:13–15; 21:6–7; Proverbs 26:15; Isaiah 44:12–20; Matthew 19:24; 23:24; and Acts 12:1–19. God laughs at the wicked in Psalm 2:7. Humor has a positive theological purpose: it enables us to see ourselves in God's perspective; it knocks us down a peg or two. It shows the ridiculous discrepancy between God's greatness and our pretensions. As such, the emotion arising from humor can pass very quickly into a deep sorrow for sin and a craving for God's grace. Humor can also express joy in the Lord and the "hilarious" cheer (2 Cor. 9:7 in the Greek) by which God's Spirit frees us from selfishness to serve our brothers and sisters. Humor can also establish a bond between leader and people, reassuring them that he is one of them. Thus, it can strengthen the horizontal side of worship, the unity of the body of Christ. Doubtless some kinds of humor are distracting in worship, but not all.

Another important consideration is that the style chosen must promote the intelligibility of the communication. We have seen that this is the chief emphasis of 1 Corinthians 14, which is the most extended treatment of a Christian worship meeting in the New Testament. Intelligibility of communication is crucial to the Great Commission and to the demand of love, for love seeks to promote, not impede, mutual understanding.

Intelligibility requires us, first, to speak the language of the people, not Latin, as the Reformers emphasized. But communication is more than language in the narrow sense. Content is communicated through body language, style, the choice of popular rather than technical terms, well-known musical styles, etc.

All in all, it seems to me that the relevant considerations favor an informal service with a friendly, welcoming atmosphere and contemporary styles in language and music. This is not a rigid or hard rule. But when we depart from this pattern, we should understand what we are doing, and we should make some effort to remedy the problems we may create.

The typical criticism of this approach is that it caters to people's tastes. Of course, the broad rules governing worship are divine commands, not people's tastes, as we have seen. But one of those divine commands is to worship in ways that are intelligible to church members and visitors. Determining the most intelligible form of worship requires us to ask what people in a particular culture most easily listen to and understand, and that question certainly overlaps the issue of taste. But we are not asking that question to satisfy anybody's taste; we are asking it so that we may be more faithful in communicating God's word clearly.

Indeed, asking such questions may force us to go against the tastes of many, notably our own! We may well have to set aside our prejudices and tastes as we plan our worship. One who loves classical music and deep theology may have to accept some contemporary choruses and childlike rhymes.[4] Worship is not merely for ourselves as individuals, but for God, for our fellow Christians, and for the unbelieving visitors (1 Cor. 14:22–25). We must distinguish between what God requires and what we are comfortable with, between scriptural standards and mere individual preferences. And in matters of individual preferences, we must be willing to consider others ahead of ourselves.

Authenticity in Worship

Often after worship, people complain that they have not really worshiped, not really met with God. Indeed, Christians sometimes attend services over long periods of time without the sense that they have really encountered the living Lord there. Occasionally something happens during worship that is deeply life-transforming. But for many of us that happens far too rarely.

Some people blame themselves for that spiritual dullness; others blame the church. I recently read an article by a friend who left the Presbyterian Church in America for an Eastern Orthodox communion. He offered the usual criticisms of evangelical Presbyterian worship: too casual, shallow, inadequately planned, insufficiently historical, not participative. He said that when he first attended a "high liturgical" service, he was amazed at the richness of it. "I felt like I had never worshiped before," he said.

So we might be tempted to think that establishing authenticity in worship means adopting a historical liturgy. But I have heard testimonies of the opposite sort as well—from people raised in Roman Catholicism or Eastern Orthodoxy who never had a personal relationship with God until they heard the gospel proclaimed simply and without ceremony in an evangelical Protestant church.[5] We must remind ourselves that God works when and where he wills. Nobody can prove from Scripture or statistics that formal worship generates depth and authenticity more than informal worship, or vice versa.

Deep experiences of God can take place under a wide variety of conditions: at a summer camp; during a family crisis; at a counseling center; in different sorts of worship. Sometimes a change from one style of worship to another can have a jarring effect, engaging the worshiper's attention to an extraordinary degree. That may be the tool the Spirit uses to deal with that worshiper, or it may merely be the situation that leads the worshiper to think that the Spirit is dealing with him in an extraordinary way.

In any case, there is no technique for insuring that such experiences will take place. All we can do is to make sure that our worship follows God's commands and to make sure that our own hearts, as worshipers, are seeking to honor the Lord. (Note the connection between purity of heart and worship in Ps. 24:4 and Matt. 5:8.) Even that will not guarantee a special feeling of God's presence for every worshiper in every service. But our worship will be authentic in the sense that most matters: it will please God and edify the congregation, and that should be enough to satisfy us as worshipers.

Questions for Discussion

1. Are you tempted to think of worship as an academic lecture? Do you see the hymns, prayers, and sacraments as mere preliminaries to the sermon? If so, what changes in the worship of your church will encourage you to think differently? What changes in your own attitude?

2. Does God address his word primarily to the intellect? Why or why not? How can the worship of your church develop a better balance?

3. Does the worship of your church encourage reverence, joy, repentance, participation, faith, love, boldness, and family intimacy? How? If not, what changes are needed? How can you encourage such attitudes in yourself and in other worshipers?

4. What different styles of worship have you experienced? Share them with the class, along with your evaluation of them.

5. Have you ever criticized worship because it does not accord with your personal taste? What was your concern—music, decor, length of time, comfort, location, or the ethnic, economic, or cultural background of the other worshipers? Have you ever been challenged to compromise your preferences for the edification of others? What was your response? Be self-critical.

6. Have you ever been affected by worship in a profound, life-changing way? Describe the experience. Do you believe that experience was connected with a particular style or atmosphere of worship? Should we expect that kind of experience in every service? Should we plan worship so as to arouse that sort of experience?

7. What would you say to someone who, after church on Sunday morning, tells you, "I didn't get much out of that service"?

Notes

[1] One cannot actually live by feelings without thought, for the two are inseparable. But there are people whose thought and decisions are

of poor quality because they are based on momentary impressions rather than careful consideration. This is what we mean when we accuse somebody of "living by feelings."

[2]See my *Doctrine of the Knowledge of God* (Phillipsburg, N.J.: Presbyterian and Reformed, 1987), 328–46, for a more extended account of the relations between intellect, will, emotions, and other human faculties.

[3]Klaas Runia describes him as "rather rationalistic" in this regard. See his "The Reformed Liturgy in the Dutch Tradition," in *Worship: Adoration and Action,* ed. Donald A. Carson (Grand Rapids: Baker, 1993), 99. The whole article is illuminating as it traces this tendency through the history of Reformed worship.

[4]This comment is somewhat autobiographical. God has had to deal with me in these areas. I studied classical piano for eight years, organ for five, plus harmony and counterpoint. And by profession I am a theologian. So by training and personal preference I favor classical music and profound theological reflection in worship. But God's word, and the prodding of some friends, has forced me to question my own prejudice in this area.

[5]Charismatic churches boast many such testimonies in their favor.

8

God Speaks to Us: The Word and the Sacraments

In the next chapters, we will be looking at some of the major aspects of worship more closely than we have so far been able to do. Earlier I rejected the notion that worship must be dialogical in the sense of a rigid structure of alternating exchanges between God and the people. Nevertheless, it is true that in worship God speaks and we respond to him. As a convenient arrangement of topics I shall in this chapter discuss some worship events in which God's speech is prominent. In the next chapter we shall consider our responses to God's word.

The Word of God

First, God speaks to us through the reading and preaching of his word in Scripture. It is important for our worship to recognize that when we hear or read the word of God, we are encountering God himself. The power of the Holy Spirit accompanies God's word (1 Cor. 2:12–15; 1 Thess. 1:5) to give us understanding.

But to say that God accompanies his word is not to tell the whole story. The relation of God to his word is even more profound than that, for the word itself is divine. We know that to agree with or criticize a man's words is to agree with or criticize him. The same is true of God. God's word is inseparable from God himself. His word performs divine acts: creation (Ps. 33:6), providence (Ps. 148), judgment (John 12:48), and salvation (Rom. 1:16; James 1:21). Everything God does, he does by speaking his word. His word has divine attributes: it is eternal (Ps. 119:89, 160), omnipotent (Isa. 55:11), and perfect (Ps. 19:7–8). It is even a proper object of worship (Pss. 119:120, 161–62; 56:4, 10).[1] Thus, the apostle John, speaking both of Jesus, the living Word, and of the creative word in Genesis 1:3 and Psalm 33:6, identifies God's word with God himself (John 1:1).

We should draw two implications from this for worship: First, where God's word is, God is. We should never take God's word for granted. To hear the word of God is to meet with God himself. Second, where God is, the word is. We should not seek to have an experience with God which bypasses or transcends his word.

God's word brings wonderful blessings upon us as we hear it in faith, with obedient hearts. But his word is also powerful to bring judgment on those who rebel or fail to take it seriously. In Isaiah 6:9–10, the word of God given to a disobedient people actually hardens them, so that they are less likely to obey and receive God's blessing. Jesus quotes this passage to explain the dual purpose of his parables: to enlighten some and hide the truth from others (Matt. 13:11–17). God's word never leaves us the same; it leaves us better or worse. Thus, it is urgent that we hear in faith.

The Reading of Scripture

The first written word of God mentioned in Scripture is the Decalogue. On two stone tablets God wrote the Ten Commandments (Ex. 24:12; 31:18; 32:15–16; 34:1, 28–32). These words were the "words of the covenant" (34:28), which set forth the laws and promises of the covenant relationship between God and Israel.[2] Over and over again, Israel was charged to obey the words, testimonies, commands, statutes, and ordinances of God's law (for this emphasis, see almost any page of Deuteronomy). God also commanded that the words of the covenant (the Decalogue along with additional words given by God) should be read and taught publicly to the people (Deut. 31–32). Similarly, the apostles expected the churches to read their letters publicly (Col. 4:16; 1 Thess. 5:27; 1 Tim. 4:13). The reading of Scripture is not just a prelude to the sermon. It is, in its own right, an act commanded by God for public worship. It is a renewal of God's covenant with us, for we hear God's promises and commands and respond in obedience. And as we hear, we expose ourselves to the Spirit's power.

Preaching and Teaching

Preaching and teaching[3] explain the Scriptures and apply them to our lives. It is through the preaching of the word that God normally brings people to believe in Jesus (Rom. 10:14ff.; 1 Cor. 1:21; 2:1–5). Preaching is therefore very important. The Second Helvetic Confession states that "the preaching of the word of God is the word of God." This statement should not be used by preachers to argue for their own infallibility! Rather, what it means is that insofar as the preacher rightly proclaims the word, his words are God's. God's word does not become something less than it is, merely by being placed on the lips of a human being. When we hear the true preaching of the word, we are confronted with the very power, authority, and awesome presence of God Himself.

An elder of the church must be "able to teach" (1 Tim. 3:2; compare Titus 1:9). Some elders are paid to focus their attention on preaching and teaching (1 Tim. 5:17). Today, these are sometimes called teaching elders or ministers as distinguished from ruling elders.

Nevertheless, teaching in the church is not restricted to elders. In the synagogue, any Jewish man could be appointed to exhort the congregation (compare Luke 4:16–19). The same practice is suggested by the language of 1 Corinthians 14:26, speaking of Christian worship meetings. Note also Hebrews 10:24–25, where every Christian is given the responsibility of edifying the body in connection with worship. In Colossians 3:16, all believers teach one another as they sing praise.

Women are not permitted to serve as elders, as we have seen. However, Paul says that older women should teach younger women (Titus 2:4–5), and Priscilla was involved with her husband Aquila in the instruction given to Apollos (Acts 18:24–28).

It is important that teaching be intelligible, clear, and edifying (1 Cor. 14). When Ezra and the Levites taught the law to Israel, the assembly consisted of those "who could understand" (Neh. 8:3). Those who could not understand, evidently, were instructed in other contexts. Some Reformed people insist that all children should be present in church during every sermon, rather than being sent off to nurseries and "children's churches." There is certainly value in families worshiping together as much as possible. God deals not only with individuals in Scripture, but also with households. The family is vitally important. In worship, however, edification (1 Cor. 14:26) is more important than mere togetherness. Ideally, everybody should be taught at his own level of understanding. I would like to see some occasions where God's people gather to hear the word presented simply, so that all can share the message together. But there should be other occasions in which the people are divided, so that everyone hears the word of God at his own level of understanding.

Drama?

Many churches are using drama today in an attempt to communicate the word of God more clearly than could be done through more traditional forms of preaching. Some Presbyterians oppose this, because there is no specific command in Scripture to use drama in this way. But we have seen that specific commands are not always needed. When God gives us a general command (in this case the command to preach the word), and is silent on some aspect of its specific application, we may properly make those applications ourselves, within the general rules of Scripture. The questions before us, then, are whether drama is legitimately a form of preaching or teaching, and whether there are any scriptural teachings that would rule it out as a means of communicating the word. I would answer yes to the first question, and no to the second.

Scripture never says that preaching and teaching must be done by monologue, although they are normally done that way. Surely there is no reason why there shouldn't be two or more teachers expounding the word at a particular meeting.

Further, biblical preaching and teaching contain many dramatic elements. At God's behest, the prophets sometimes performed symbolic actions, as in Ezekiel 4:1–15 and chapter 5. Jesus often taught through dialogue, with both friendly and unfriendly parties. He taught by parables, which often included dialogues between different characters, Jesus playing all the roles, as in Luke 12:13–21; 16:19–31; 18:1–8. Paul's letters, too, are often dramatic, with Paul carrying on dialogues with his questioners, objectors, and accusers. And the book of Revelation is a dramatic feast. These dramatic elements must be emphasized whenever we preach on these texts; otherwise we miss important aspects of their content.

God often teaches his people through drama. The book of Job, the Old Testament sacrifices[4] and feasts, and the New Testament sacraments are reenactments of God's great works of redemption. As we have seen, the traditional liturgy has continued this process of reenactment for many centuries, so drama in worship is nothing new.

If we grant that the word can be preached or taught by more than one speaker, that teaching can take place through dialogue, and that teaching inevitably has dramatic elements, then we cannot object to drama as a form of teaching.

I am not an advocate of the use of drama. In my view, there

are many considerations arguing that the word is usually presented better through the traditional monologue than through drama. Dramas are hard to write, plan, and rehearse. When done poorly, they are a distraction, and when done well (usually by professional leadership), the cost exceeds the value of the performance. And perhaps especially now, amid all the technological and media clutter, it can be refreshing and powerful to receive a straightforward "live" message from one man entrusted with the word of God, speaking from the heart as "a dying man to dying men." The simplicity of such an address can have, as our Puritan fathers emphasized, a great spiritual power. Nevertheless, I do believe that Scripture gives us the freedom to use drama; we may not dogmatically restrict the proclamation of the word in worship to the traditional monologue form.

In my experience, dramas are most effective in worship when they pose a question to which the sermon presents a scriptural answer.

Blessings

Another way in which God addresses the congregation is through the pronouncement of blessing. At the beginning of worship, the blessing is usually called a salutation or greeting. The letters of Paul typically contain near the beginning a blessing and greeting, such as "Grace and peace to you from God our Father and from the Lord Jesus Christ" (Rom. 1:7), and in worship services such language is typically used in the greeting. At the end of worship, customarily, the pastor pronounces a benediction, such as the Aaronic benediction of Numbers 6:22–27 or the apostolic benediction of 2 Corinthians 13:14.

In the blessing, God identifies the people as his own, placing his own name upon them, and promises anew the blessings of the gospel.

Scripture nowhere commands the church to use these formulas in public worship. Nevertheless, their content is biblical; indeed, they amount simply to additional Scripture readings. Further, it is certainly appropriate for God's people, when gathered in the name of Christ, to receive a blessing that identifies them as God's own.

Censures

If worship includes God's blessing on his people, may it also include his censure upon those who have betrayed the covenant? I believe so. We saw in chapter 5 that church discipline is a proper aspect of worship. What we should understand here is that when the church pronounces a judicial censure (admonition, rebuke, deposition from office, or excommunication), it is applying the word of God. When rightly done, a censure is God's word, spoken to the offender and to the congregation.

Jesus teaches in Matthew 18:18 (in a context of discipline) that what the church binds on earth is bound in heaven. This does not mean that the church's judgments are infallible. It does mean that when the church's judgments are just, when they properly bind offenders, they represent God's judgment as well. Similarly, the apostle Paul says that even when the apostle is absent, the church's judgments have just as much authority as when the apostle is present (1 Cor. 5:3–5).

Calls to Worship

There are in Scripture many passages in which God calls or summons his people to worship him, such as Psalms 95:1–7; 96:1–3; 100:1. Like the greeting and the benediction, the call to worship is a reading of Scripture for a particular purpose. And, like the blessings, there is no biblical command to have a call to worship in every service. Some have put great emphasis on the necessity of a call to worship (and also a dismissal at the end) because they wish to draw a sharp distinction between "official worship" and any other sort of gathering. Since I reject that sharp distinction, I don't believe it is necessary to have a formal, explicit call to worship in every service. Nevertheless, it is good to remind people of the meeting's purpose. That reminding can be done through a hymn, a prayer, an exhortation, or by a formal call to worship.

Sacraments

Protestants are often confused about the meaning and point of their two sacraments, baptism and the Lord's Supper. We don't believe what Roman Catholics believe, but what is the positive alternative?

In Reformed theology, the sacraments are signs and seals of the covenant of grace. That is to say, they symbolize our salvation, and they promise it to us in Christ. Baptism symbolizes cleansing from sin; the Lord's Supper proclaims the Lord's death until he comes (1 Cor. 11:26). By these ordinances, God identifies us as his people and binds us to one another in Christ.

These blessings are the same as those given in the reading and preaching of the word of God. As we have seen, the word also symbolizes the truth of the gospel and seals the promise by God's guarantee. God himself, the Holy Spirit, comes to us in and with the word to seal it to our hearts. That word also renews God's covenant with us, identifying us as the people of God. Therefore, the Reformers often described the sacraments as "visible words." What the word presents to our hearing, the sacraments present to our eyes, and also to our other physical senses. The content is the same; the medium is different.[5]

To call the sacraments "visible words" may seem to trivialize them, unless we recall what a great and wonderful thing the word of God is. The word is God; it is his presence with us; it is Jesus Christ ministering to us in the Holy Spirit. It is in that way that Christ is "present" in the Lord's Supper, and, indeed, in baptism too. The water of baptism is only water, and the bread and wine are only bread and wine; no magical changes take place when these are used in the sacraments. We should not bow down to them or bow to the table on which they are placed. But because the sacraments are visible words, they are also a "participation" (1 Cor. 10:16–17) in Christ, and of the worshipers with one another in him.

The symbolism of the sacraments is very rich—hard to summarize in a sentence or two, although I did attempt such a summary early in this section. Baptism symbolizes cleansing, but it also symbolizes the ordeal of threatening waters (the divine judgment) through which God brings his people.[6] The Lord's Supper recalls the Old Testament Passover, the fellowship offerings of the temple, the manna by which God fed his people in the wilderness, and the fruitful harvests by which God fed his people in the Promised Land. It points us both to the past and to the future—to the death of Christ for our sins, in the light of the promise of his coming again (1 Cor. 11:26). And in the present it nourishes our souls (John 6:48–59). The elements represent the body and blood of Christ, given for us in sacrifice; they also represent the body of Christ in another sense: the church assembled for worship (1 Cor. 10:17; compare 11:17–22, 27–29).

As with the word, there is blessing in the sacraments, but also the potential of curse. Receiving baptism and the Lord's Supper unites one with Christ, his church, and his purposes. Those who have identified themselves with the church, and then turn away, face a judgment worse than those who never professed Christ (Luke 12:47–48; Heb. 6:4–6; 10:26–31). Those who receive the Lord's Supper unworthily may come under serious judgment; they may even get sick and die (1 Cor. 11:27–34).

Therefore, Paul tells us to examine ourselves before we eat (v. 28). This self-examination should not be a microscopic analysis of all our sins and hidden motives, as if only perfect people could receive the sacrament. In the context of 1 Corinthians 11, it has to do with the sin of despising other worshipers. We need not be sinless to take the sacrament; the Lord's Supper is for sinners. Its message is the gospel of salvation from sin. But to take the Lord's Supper signifies our commitment to flee from sin, and God will hold us responsible for that. If we are not sensitive to the sort of rebuke that Paul gave the Corinthians in 1 Corinthians 11, then we should not partake of the sacrament.

The blessings of the sacraments, then, are not automatic. Those blessings, like the blessings of the word, must be received by faith.

Infant Baptism

The importance of faith raises a question about infant baptism, which is the practice in Reformed and Presbyterian churches. It might be argued that an infant cannot receive baptism by faith, since he or she does not have adequate understanding. I cannot enter into the full argument for infant baptism here, but note the following:

1. In the Old Testament, infants clearly received the sign of the covenant, the sign that identified them as God's people (Gen. 17:1–14). Under the Old Covenant, that sign was circumcision; in the New Covenant, it is baptism (see Col. 2:11–12). All the arguments against infant baptism count equally against infant circumcision. But they clearly fail in the latter case, and so they fail in the former as well.

2. Jesus laid his hands upon infants to bless them (Mark 10:13–16). As we have seen, the blessing identifies a person with God and with the covenant people. It places the name of God upon them. This is the essence of baptism. If the blessing is appropriate for infants, baptism is also.

3. In Scripture, God deals not only with individuals, but with families, churches, and nations. That is plain in the Old Testament. But also in the New Testament, salvation—and baptism—comes not only to individuals, but to households as well (Acts 2:39; 11:14; 16:15, 31). Whether there were or were not infants in these households is irrelevant. When a first-century Jew heard about households being baptized, he would surely have related that to the Old Testament pattern he knew so well: parents and children together receiving the sign of God's covenant. Household baptisms suggest that that pattern was unchanged. If there had been a change, it would have been taught explicitly, and some explanation would have been given for the persistence of "household" language.

Infants, therefore, do rightly receive baptism. How, then, does faith enter the picture in their case? Their parents exercise faith by bringing their household to God. When children reach the age of understanding, they must take responsibility for their position among the people of God. They, too, must believe and obey the Lord, or else be excluded from God's people.[7]

Questions for Discussion

1. Why is it so momentous and solemn for us to hear the word of God? Why do we so often take it casually? How can we avoid that temptation for ourselves and help our fellow worshipers to take the word more seriously?
2. "By the word and the sacraments, God renews his covenant with us." Explain.
3. Does your congregation have a "children's church"? Discuss whether this is right or wrong according to Scripture.
4. Have you been in services where dramas have been performed? Did those enhance or detract from the worship? Why? What biblical principles should govern our decisions on this issue?
5. What does it mean to say that a sacrament is a "sign"? A "seal"? How is Christ present in the sacraments?
6. "The word and the sacraments are powerful means of blessing and of judgment." Explain.
7. What role does faith play in the reception of God's blessing through the word and the sacraments? Should we reject infant baptism because an infant cannot exercise faith? Discuss.

Notes

[1]Of course, we must be cautious in stating this point. To say that the word is an object of worship is not to endorse bibliolatry—bowing down before the paper and ink of Scripture. Nevertheless, we should respond to God's word in Scripture with the same obedience and deference—and worship—by which we would respond to God's personal appearance.

[2]See Meredith G. Kline, *The Structure of Biblical Authority* (Grand Rapids: Eerdmans, 1972). In this impressive work, Kline shows the role of the "covenant document" within the overall covenant relationship. This is the most important defense of biblical authority since B. B. Warfield.

[3]Scripture does not, in my view, draw a sharp distinction between these.

[4]Since the animal sacrifices did not take away sin, but pointed to the future atoning work of Christ, their function was essentially dramatic.

[5]The phrase "visible words" does have a liability. It might suggest to some that the main purpose of the sacraments is for us to sit and gaze at them. That would, of course, encourage a passive, even idolatrous disposition in the worshiper. It is important, therefore, to emphasize that the sacraments are not only visible words, but also words that can be touched, smelled, and tasted.

[6]See Meredith G. Kline, *By Oath Consigned* (Grand Rapids: Eerdmans, 1968).

[7]In this book I am avoiding the parallel question of whether infants or small children should be admitted to the Lord's Supper (paedocommunion). However, my inclination is to say that the two are similar. Small children cannot examine themselves (1 Cor. 11:28), but they cannot repent and believe either (Acts 2:38). It is reasonable to say that both of these passages are addressed to adults and do not set forth requirements for all recipients of the sacraments.

9

We Speak to God: Our Response to God's Word

In this chapter, we shall consider the congregation's response to God's word. We should be reminded again, however, that there is no sharp distinction between the aspects of worship mentioned in the last chapter and those discussed here. In worship, God should always be speaking to us, since the whole content of worship should be scriptural. And we should be constantly responding to that word in faith and obedience.

Prayer

The Westminster Shorter Catechism defines prayer as "an offering up of our desires unto God, for things agreeable to his will, in the name of Christ, with confession of our sins, and thankful acknowledgment of his mercies" (Q. 98). This definition includes the elements of request, confession of sin, and thanksgiving. We should, I believe, add the element of praise—not only for God's "mercies" to us, but also for his greatness as God.[1] In all these aspects, prayer is part of public worship.[2] Let us consider each aspect.

1. *Praise (Adoration).* In Scripture, God's people often pray to acknowledge his divine nature: his eternity, wisdom, power, love, mercy, and justice. Since worship is homage, the very essence of worship is praise—telling God how wonderful he is. All of worship should be praise in the sense that in everything we acknowledge him as Lord.

2. *Requests (Supplication).* The main rule for requests is that they should be made "in Jesus' name" (John 14:13–14; 15:16; 16:23–26). To pray "in Jesus' name" is to pray as a disciple, as Jesus' servant and friend. When we pray in Jesus' name, we pray for what is pleasing to him, not primarily for what will make us happy. In 1 John 5:14, a favorable answer is promised to anyone who prays "according to his will." This suggests to me a close relationship between prayer in Jesus' name and prayer according to his will. In prayer, as in all worship, we seek what pleases the Lord, not what pleases ourselves.

Of course, we know that Jesus loves us and wants us to be happy. That fact is relevant for prayer, as it is for worship in general. One day he will make us ecstatic with unending joy. But the road to that happiness is often paved with suffering, as we follow his footsteps to the cross. Our prayers must accept his will in that regard as in all others. With Jesus himself, we should pray, "Yet not as I will, but as you will" (Matt. 26:39).

We should, therefore, always seek to conform our prayers to the word of God. We should pray for the blessings that God has promised us.[3] What of things that God has not specifically promised in Scripture? Is it right to pray for a job, healing of a particular illness, or an opportunity to share the gospel with a neighbor? Certainly it is, as long as our prayer does not arise from a sinful desire. Jesus prayed that somehow it might not be necessary for him to suffer on the cross (Matt. 26:39). That was a godly desire; it is right for us to seek relief from pain and suffering. In that sense, such a prayer is in God's will. But God, in his higher purposes, does not always grant relief from suffering (compare 2 Cor. 12:7–10).

There are wonderful promises in Scripture to those who

pray in Jesus' name, but often, as we've seen, God says no. Does God's no contradict Jesus' promise, "You may ask me for anything in my name, and I will do it" (John 14:14)? Here we should keep two principles in mind: First, God's no is only temporary. Every godly prayer will be answered in the glory of the new heavens and the new earth. In that kingdom, every disease will be healed, all of God's elect will be saved, and God's people will live as kings. Second, if the ultimate prayer of our hearts is that God's will be done, and if we are willing to hold loosely to our specific concerns for the overall good of the kingdom (Matt. 6:33), then even in this world our prayers will always be answered.

3. *Confession of Sin.* When we approach God in prayer, we should approach him not only as servants, but also as sinners saved by grace. We have offended God; we can approach him only in Jesus' name—only on the basis of his shed blood.

Although God forgives our sins once for all in Christ, we may not forget about sin as we approach God's presence. We must remember and honor the sacrifice of Christ as the basis on which we come to God. And we must admit that we continue to sin every day (1 John 1:8–10). The sins of Christians are not less grievous to God than those of unbelievers. If we love Jesus, we too will grieve over our sins; we will be sorry that we have displeased him. And we will regularly admit our sins and ask God's forgiveness for the sake of Jesus.

Sincere confession involves repentance. Repentance is more than feeling sorry for sin, more even than asking for forgiveness. It is an actual turning from sin. It is behavioral, not just mental. If we come to God claiming that we hate our sin and desire to be rid of it through Jesus, then at the same time we must have the serious purpose of forsaking that sin; otherwise, our confession is only words.

4. *Thanksgiving.* Every good gift comes from God in heaven (James 1:16). To God we owe everything that we are and everything that we have. God owes us nothing; all our blessings come to us because of his kindness. Indeed, since as sinners we deserve

only death and endless punishment, God's blessings come to us by grace—his unmerited favor.

Therefore, as the Heidelberg Catechism teaches, the entire Christian life is thanksgiving—a grateful response to God's kindness. To be thankless is to despise God's blessings—indeed, it is to despise *him*.

Therefore, biblical prayer abounds in thanks for all the blessings of God. God's people rejoice even in suffering, as did the apostles after they had been flogged, "because they had been counted worthy of suffering disgrace for the Name" (Acts 5:41; compare Phil. 3:10; Col. 1:24; 1 Peter 1:6–9; 4:13). We do not give thanks *for* sickness, pain, Satan, and sin. But we thank God for his good purposes in allowing these into our lives—good purposes that will in his time lead to the end of all our sin and suffering.

Confessions of Faith

There are many passages of Scripture that contain brief summaries of our faith, such as Deuteronomy 6:4–5; Romans 1:3–4; 4:24–25; 1 Corinthians 15:3–5. Deuteronomy 6:4–5 (with other passages) has long been recited by the congregation in the synagogue as a public profession of the faith of Israel. In the Christian church, there have also been occasions for such confession. The baptism of adults involves a public confession of repentance and faith (Acts 2:38), and historically Christian congregations have used various creeds in public worship to identify themselves as God's people. Passages of Scripture have been used for this purpose, as have ancient formulations such as the Apostles' Creed and the Nicene Creed.

There is no command in Scripture to include creeds as part of public worship, but even the strictest advocates of the regulative principle have included them. On the approach I have suggested, creeds may be seen as applications of the commandment to read and teach the word. A creed is simply the church's statement of what it believes the Scriptures teach. Further, when people meet in the name of Christ, it is altogether fitting that they identify themselves as his people. A creed does that, by setting forth the gospel.

I do not believe that every worship service must include the recitation of a creed. The purpose of such recitation (summarizing the gospel, identifying ourselves as God's people) may be accomplished in other ways—by hymns, prayers, teaching, and the sacraments. Nevertheless, reciting the historic creeds is one very useful way to instruct people on the basics of the word of God. And it promotes the unity of the body by identifying everyone with the church's foundation in God's word.

Congregational Responses

In Psalm 136, each verse concludes with the words, "His love endures forever." It appears that in worship this psalm was recited antiphonally: one leader or group would speak the first part of the verse, and then other speakers would respond, "His love endures forever." Some other psalms may also have antiphonal elements.

The word *amen*, "so may it stand," is a frequent response in Scripture. In Deuteronomy 27, Moses told the people to respond with "Amen" to a recitation of curses on those who commit various sins. Thus Israel acknowledged that disobedience rightly deserves God's awful judgment (see also 1 Chron. 16:36; Neh. 5:13; 8:6; Ps. 106:48; Matt. 28:20; Rom. 1:25). "Amen" was not a routine ending to prayers and hymns, as it is in many churches today; many psalms and prayers in Scripture do not end with it. But Scripture often uses the term to reinforce its teaching and as a means for us to express our enthusiastic agreement with what God says to us.

Many other statements from Scripture and church tradition have been used as congregational responses, to encourage a greater level of participation. Here are two examples.

> LEADER: The Lord be with you.
> PEOPLE: And with your spirit.

LEADER: Lift up your hearts.
PEOPLE: We lift them up unto the Lord.

Insofar as these responses are scriptural in content, they are legitimate. However, Scripture does not command us to use them in public worship. If we do use them, we must do so as a way of applying more general biblical principles, such as the command to teach and edify one another, the command to participate in worship, and so on. We must bear in mind that the purposes of these responses, like the purposes of creeds, can be fulfilled in other ways.

Many of the responsive sentences from church tradition have become rather obscure to modern congregations, and to repeat the same sentences over and over again from week to week can defeat the goal of meaningful, alert participation. The same can be said for congregational prayers that have been written out. Churches that use such responsive forms should take pains to use forms that are currently understandable (1 Cor. 14, again) and to vary them sufficiently that they do not become dead formalities.

Individual Participation

Some traditional Puritan and Presbyterian theologians have insisted that only an elder may speak extemporaneously in worship. On this view, the other members of the congregation may only speak together in unison, which requires a "script," that is, hymns, responsive sentences, etc., whose words have been written out. This position is based on the argument that only an elder may "lead" in worship, an argument that I discussed and rejected in chapter 6.

On my view, however, members of the congregation may speak or sing in worship, not only in unison and by script, but individually as well. Indeed, this kind of broad participation is assumed in 1 Corinthians 14:26. Certainly, this participation must be done in an orderly way; that is Paul's precise concern in 1 Corinthians 14. That means that the elders must oversee the service carefully, doing their best to maintain order, promote edification, and prevent deviations from biblical truth and practice.

Nevertheless, there is no reason why individual members, in submission to the elders, should not be permitted to (1) give individual testimonies of what God has done in their lives, for which the congregation can give thanks, (2) offer requests for congregational prayer, (3) lead in prayer themselves, (4) teach songs to the congregation or present songs for congregational meditation, (5) ask questions about the teaching of the word, and (6) offer insights arising from their own Bible study. Often such practices will be edifying and will enhance the worship of the congregation.

I believe that worship of this sort is participative in a more serious sense than worship that merely asks the congregation to utter scripted responses. However, it is good to offer opportunities for scripted response as well, for that will encourage participation by people who lack the ability or maturity to participate in more individual ways, and it will underscore the unity of the body.

Of course, in the deepest sense, participation includes not only the things we say and sing, but especially the way we think during worship. One can attend a service designed to include all sorts of participation without actually participating in it. In the final analysis, we participate by paying attention and involving ourselves in the worship. If we do not accept this responsibility, we may not blame the church's liturgy for our failure to participate.

In the end, whether people participate or not depends on what God does in their hearts. Pastors and elders can encourage participation in various ways. But I am inclined to think that the most successful ways are not the ones you read about in the worship literature. While scripted responses and opportunities for individual presentations can be helpful, I tend to think that the best incentives for participation are spirit-filled preaching and prayer. It is when God reaches our hearts through worship that we truly sense that we have been part of it, that we have participated.[4]

Questions for Discussion

1. What is prayer? What are the major kinds of prayer? Which are most neglected in your own prayer life? In the worship of your church?
2. Does your church recite a creed during worship? Why or why not? Should all churches do this? Why or why not?
3. Have you been to a "high church" service with many scripted congregational responses? Did you feel that this practice helped your worship or detracted from it? Why? What effect do such liturgies have upon visitors from outside such traditions?
4. What are some of the dangers in individual participation? How should elders guard against such dangers? What are the dangers of not permitting such participation?
5. Try to remember an occasion when you felt that you really participated in worship. What was the service like? Were there aspects of it that aroused your participation, or was it simply the working of God's Spirit in your heart? If something in the service encouraged you to participate, describe it.

Notes

[1]The writers of the catechism, of course, were well aware of the importance of praise. Their own prayers are full of adoration, recalling the praises of the Psalms. I believe they did not include praise specifically in their definition of prayer because in their day the term *prayer* was used rather narrowly to refer to requests or petitions. Of course, even praise can be understood as a kind of petition, as in Question 101, where "Hallowed be thy name" is interpreted as a petition asking God to glorify himself. Since any prayer of ours must be granted by God, there is a sense in which all prayer is petition. There is also a sense in which all prayer is praise, seeking to honor the Lord.

[2]The well-known acronym ACTS is helpful in remembering these main aspects of prayer: Adoration, Confession, Thanksgiving, and Supplication.

[3]People sometimes say that when God has promised something, we should not pray for it, since prayer in that case would indicate doubt or unbelief that God will keep his promise. But that reasoning

is quite unscriptural. Many, perhaps most, prayers in Scripture are for things that God has promised. Consider the Lord's Prayer: every petition is for something God has promised us.

[4]For consideration of the offering and "expressions of fellowship" as congregational responses to the word of God, see chap. 5.

10

Music in Worship

Music in worship is a large topic, fraught with controversy today. Therefore, I have postponed discussion of it until this point, so that we might discuss it at some length.

Why Music?

Scripture plainly teaches that God's people are not only to speak, but also to sing, the truth of God (e.g., 1 Chron. 16:9; Ps. 33:2–3; Col. 3:16). So, music is an important part of worship.

Why is this? Why music, rather than, say, waving banners, shooting off fireworks, or sitting in yoga positions?

Music is closely related to the spoken word. Human speech has a kind of natural music about it: rhythm, timbre, and pitch play important roles in verbal communication, and not only in tonal languages. In one sense, then, all language is musical. When we enhance that natural music with well-crafted melodies, harmonies, and instruments, our words often take on a new kind of vitality.

I will speak of all verbal communication being musical in a

111

"broad sense." Speech enhanced by prominent use of melody, harmony, and rhythm will be music in a "narrow sense." In that narrow sense, melody, harmony, and rhythm become prominent carriers of meaning. In this book, "music," "musical," and of course "song" will refer to the narrow sense unless otherwise noted.

What I have said about language in general applies also to the word of God. Even when being read or proclaimed, the word of God has musical characteristics. But God calls us on occasion to enhance it with music in the narrow sense. He calls us to sing his praise and to express it on musical instruments.[1] It is evident that much biblical poetry, especially in the book of Psalms (but not only there; see, e.g., Ex. 15; Deut. 32), was originally written to be sung.

Poetic and/or musical form enhance the word of God in various ways. In particular, poetic-musical forms[2] impart vividness and memorability to God's words. That vividness and memorability, in turn, drive the word into our hearts, so that it becomes precious to us and motivates us to praise and obedience.

The earliest poetry in Scripture appears at the creation of man in Genesis 1:27.[3] Poetic-musical language also appears at the institution of marriage (Gen. 2:23), the giving of curses and redemptive promises (Gen. 3:14–18), Lamech's prideful and murderous boasts (Gen. 4:23–24), God's covenants with Noah (Gen. 8:22; 9:6, 25–27), Abraham (Gen. 12:2–3), and Hagar (Gen. 16:11–12), Isaac's blessing of Jacob (Gen. 27:27–29) and Esau (Gen. 27:39–40), and Jacob's blessing on his sons (Gen. 49). In Exodus, Moses supplements the prose account of Israel's deliverance from Egypt with a song (Ex. 15). Later, God gives to Israel a song, which is to be his witness against them when they break the covenant given through Moses (Deut. 32). Thus begins a long history of redemptive songs conveying God's revelation.

The use of music revealed in these examples is very different from the typical uses of music in contemporary society. In our time, we tend to see music mainly as entertainment, or perhaps as "art for art's sake." Matters of historical importance, however, like congressional bills and international treaties, are always

written in prose. To put them into poetry or music would seem
to trivialize them. It would, indeed, be ludicrous for a president
of the United States to sing a new treaty agreement. But the use
of song for this purpose would not have seemed odd in the ancient world. Then, the most important things were commonly
expressed in poetry and music. So we see that God's word is typically poetic when something of great, lasting importance is taking place: the establishment of institutions, covenant promises,
blessings and curses, and prophecies (and the mockery of them
by unbelievers such as Lamech).

Part of the reason for this is that in ancient Near Eastern
societies, there was less literacy and less distribution of written
texts than we have today. In such a society, most people's access
to important documents was through the memory. And, as we
have seen, poetry and music aid the memory by presenting words
vividly and in easily remembered form.

We may not conclude, however, that song in worship becomes less important in a print-oriented society. The pervasive-
ness of print and other media may lessen the importance of
song in some areas, such as civil government. But the vividness
and memorability of song continue to be important in the worship of God. God is not interested only in getting his word into
our hands; he wants to get it into our hearts (Pss. 1; 119:11, 34,
36, 69, etc.; Col. 3:16). That is the more profound reason for the
emphasis on music in biblical worship. And the need of people
for such a heart knowledge of God's word is as great today as it
was during the Old Testament period. Perhaps it is even more
difficult to achieve today amid the din of media voices. Thus, we
need the tool of music more than ever.

Music, then, enhances God's word by making it more vivid
and memorable, by driving it into our very hearts.[4] Many references to music in Scripture are found in connection with periods of revival in Israel (1 Chron. 16; 2 Chron. 15; 23; 29; 35). In
church history, too, revival usually produces new waves of music
for the church. Salvation and praise go together. God's salvation
purifies our lips and opens our mouths to sing his praise (Pss.
51:14–15; 12; Isa. 6; Zeph. 3:9–13).

However, we should not limit the importance of music to its effect on people. There is, to be sure, a horizontal dimension in worship: we do meet to edify one another. But the vertical dimension is preeminent: we worship to honor God. Music is especially important in worship, then, because God delights in it. We know he loves it because he commands us to make music. He delights in the vividness and memorability with which music conveys his word. He delights when believers have that deep heart-knowledge of himself which music encourages. And he delights in the melodies, harmonies, timbres, and rhythms themselves, for he created them to glorify himself and to edify his people.

One of the most wonderful things that Scripture says about music is that when we sing, the Lord Jesus is singing with us (see Ps. 22:22; Zeph. 3:17; Rom. 15:9). Our God is a singing Lord, one who joins us and leads us in triumphant song.

To summarize: the function of music is to glorify God by investing his word with the vividness and memorability that by his grace drives that word into the heart.

What Does Music Do?

Within its general function of glorifying God, music has many specific functions, as we can see from the Psalms and Paul's letters: praise (Pss. 8; 147–150), thanksgiving (Pss. 50:14; 100:4), supplication (Ps. 5:1–3), confession of sin (Ps. 51), confession of faith (1 Tim. 3:16), lament (Pss. 6; 10; 137), pronouncement of blessing (Pss. 4:6; 80:3, 7, 19; 86:16), and teaching (Ps. 1; Col. 3:16). Music is not an "element" of worship, distinct from all others; it is a way of doing other things.[5] It can impart vividness and memorability to any aspect of worship. I see no reason why some worship services should not be entirely musical. But biblical precedents concerning teaching, preaching, and prayer suggest that nonmusical treatment of God's word is also appropriate. The powerful tool of music should be used with some discretion and nuance. Or perhaps we should say that we should employ in worship both the richness of literal music and the simple, yet quasi-musical qualities of prose speech.

Why Is It So Controversial Today?

Why is music such a controversial matter in the contemporary church? One reason is simply that music is a basic aspect of worship. If in the broad sense music permeates worship, and if in the narrow sense God provides it to drive the word into our hearts, something vital is lost when music goes wrong. One might say that when music goes wrong, everything goes wrong. This is especially true in view of the connection we have drawn between music and the relationship of our hearts to God. When music distracts us, instead of enhancing that relationship, something vital is lost.

Controversy over music has waxed and waned over the history of the church. Of course, the words of hymns have often been a matter of contention, since hymn texts have reflected the church's theological wars. Churches have also fought battles over the tunes of hymns, and over the use of instruments, choirs, and soloists—controversies that we shall consider later on.

Besides these issues, controversies over music in modern American Presbyterianism reflect the traditional Christian ambivalence toward "popular" worship, the traditional Presbyterian ambivalence toward revival, aesthetic concerns about musical quality, and the familiar sociological pattern of the generation gap.[6]

Periods of revival, when great numbers of people profess Christ and believers are renewed in their faith, almost always produce new developments in hymnody. The Protestant Reformation produced new hymns on the Lutheran side and new psalm arrangements on the Calvinist side. Both Lutherans and Calvinists borrowed musical styles and occasionally whole tunes from secular sources. They chose words in vernacular languages, rather than Latin. Because of their rhythmic character, the psalm tunes of Louis Bourgeois were sometimes disparaged as "Geneva jigs." One might say that the Protestant Reformation led to the use of a more popular style of music in worship. It was important to the Reformers (as to the apostle Paul in Rom. 14) that worship be intelligible and meaningful to the worshipers, as well as honoring to God. Predictably, of course, people outside the Reformation movement sometimes argued that the new music was irreverent.

The evangelical awakening of the 1700s, led by the Wesleys and George Whitefield, produced a great outpouring of new music, written by Charles Wesley, Augustus Toplady, and others. These hymns tended to stress the personal experience of redemption more than the older hymns did, though of course reference to such experience in worship is as old as the Psalms. Think of "And Can It Be That I Should Gain" and "Rock of Ages, Cleft for Me." Some Presbyterians, however, resisted the new music, either on the ground that psalms alone are appropriate for worship, or as part of their general resistance to revivalism. Many of them thought that these hymns, like the revivalist preachers, were too subjective, too popular in musical style, and not doctrinally reliable.

Similar controversies developed over the outpouring of evangelical music in the late-nineteenth century (by Fanny Crosby, Ira Sankey, Frances Havergal, Philip Bliss, and others). Again, in this music there was a turning to the popular musical styles of the time and to the contemporary ways of expressing emotion. The criticisms of this music were essentially the same as the earlier criticisms: too popular, too subjective, doctrinally imprecise, impoverished, or worse.

Following World War II, there were new organizations seeking to evangelize young people, such as Youth for Christ and Young Life. This movement produced another body of songs that employed the popular musical styles of the time and the language of contemporary youth. Oldsters were often appalled. Again, in the 1970s, many participants in the counterculture of the 1960s came to profess Christ. This movement produced "Scripture songs," "choruses," and some longer hymns, in the popular musical styles of that time. Their music was criticized for essentially the same reasons, and that criticism continues to the present. When there is another revival, bringing another large group of people into the church, the music of that generation will also be brought in, once again offending older generations.

These cycles of change and reaction have occurred throughout history, but they do seem to have occurred more often in recent times. Perhaps the pace of change has increased because of modern communications: as new ideas get around more quickly, older styles of music more rapidly wear out their welcome. Further, the church has been unable to resist the cultural trend of new generations to proudly assert their own superior wisdom on all matters, rather than to defer to their elders. That tendency has always been present in the human race, but recent cultural trends and the overall decrease of Christian influence in society have intensified this problem. That problem, in turn, has accelerated change in fashions—in music as well as in many other fields.

I would suggest the following responses to these historical developments:

1. To a certain extent, these developments in church music legitimately reflect the biblical and Reformation principle that worship is to be intelligible, and therefore vernacular, and in one sense "popular" (1 Cor. 14). If the church takes this principle seriously, it will necessarily encourage changes in musical styles and language in order to communicate with new generations.

2. Such change, however, can be painful to some. To younger generations, it represents an increase in intelligibility, but to older generations, it may represent a loss. Some complaints of the older generations may be petty, creating unnecessary conflict over matters of musical taste, but generally their complaints are more serious than that. One's hymnody is his language of worship; it is the language of his heart's conversation with God. To lose the hymns one has grown up singing is, therefore, no small thing. The younger generations should learn to sympathize with this sense of loss and to accommodate their desires to the spiritual needs of their fathers and mothers in Christ. But the opposite is also true: if the older do not bend somewhat, the younger will be deprived of their own language of worship—those forms of God's word intelligible to them, by which they can best grow in Christ.[7] In this respect, both sides should defer to one another in love, in the Spirit of Christ (Matt. 20:20-26).

3. Subjectivity in hymns is not wrong in itself. Consider the extensive use of "I" and "we" in the Psalms. As I argued earlier, there is a horizontal as well as a vertical dimension in worship: in worship we are called upon both to glorify God and to edify one another. It is quite proper in worship to reflect upon one's experience with God or upon one's spiritual state. As we have seen, one of the central functions of music is to encourage religion of the heart. And indeed, that focus on individual salvation has been central to Protestant worship since the Reformation. But, of course, that perspective should not overshadow our primary focus on God's glory.

4. Concern for theological orthodoxy is entirely legitimate. Worship songs must always be biblical in content. When hymns in new styles violate theological norms, however, the proper response is not to abandon the new style, but to produce (or edit) hymns in that style that are biblically sound. We should also try to be reasonable and fair in our evaluation of the theological content of hymns, in the following respects: (a) We should remember that hymns are poetry, not prose. We should not insist that a hymn state doctrines in perfectly literal terms. (b) It is wrong to insist that a hymn say everything about a particular topic. Scripture itself, in individual passages, does not meet that requirement.

5. Concern for theological "richness" is more ambiguous. New movements in hymnody tend toward simplification at first, and as they develop further, they produce more complex poetry and music. (This is also true to some extent of the history of music in general.) Thus, at any point in history, the older style of hymnody will appear to be richer than the newer style.[8] However, there is a legitimate place in worship for both complex and simple hymns: compare Psalms 68, 69, and 119, on the one hand, with Psalms 23, 117, 131, and 133, on the other. Furthermore, it is important, in the interest of liturgical intelligibility, to adjust the level of complexity to the intellectual and spiritual maturity of the congregation. There are dangers in using highly complex, theologically rich songs in services aimed at non-Christian visitors, for example. Finally, this issue in general pre-

sents another opportunity for the older and the younger to defer to one another in love.

6. Concern for "musical quality" also requires some careful thought. I am not a musical relativist: certainly Bach's B Minor Mass is objectively better music than "Standing on the Promises." And the question of musical quality is not irrelevant to worship, since our praises are a kind of sacrificial offering that we present to God (Heb. 13:15).[9] However, objective musical quality is not the only consideration in the choice of music.[10] We must also consider the appropriateness of its text, the relation of text to tune, and the "musical languages" intelligible to the worshipers. Also, judgments regarding musical quality should not be made hastily. Many people have told me, for example, that contemporary Scripture songs and choruses in general are musically inferior. However, in my opinion, that is too broad a generalization. Some recent songs of this type are, in my estimation, equal in musical quality to any hymns of earlier traditions.[11]

The same considerations, of course, apply to questions about poetic or literary quality.

7. Concern for reverence and joy in worship is also biblically legitimate (Heb. 12:28). However, it is interesting that the music of younger generations always tends to be criticized by older generations as irreverent, while the music of older generations tends to be criticized by younger generations as lacking joy and vitality. And these generation gaps parallel similar ones in secular musical circles. These recurring patterns suggest that some of our complaints may be based on factors other than a proper zeal for God.

We must remind ourselves that just as human languages differ in the way they express common meanings, so there are differences in "musical languages." Some traditions express joy largely in major keys and fast speeds, while others do not. Some traditions express reverence only at slow tempos, while others are not so limited. Perhaps some of this has to do with the fact that younger people tend to have more energy and liveliness than their elders. In any case, it is not as easy as we sometimes think to identify music as being flat-out irreverent (or as lacking joy).

This is not to say that we shouldn't give the matter some attention. At least within a particular subculture we can usually identify some music that would be understood by all reasonable Christians as irreverent (or joyless) in a particular context. Such music should of course be avoided.

Music in worship is one of God's best tools for getting the word into our hearts. In a mysterious way, our own decisions about worship songs are also important. God wants us to make these decisions in a way that embraces his own purposes for music, and therefore speaks the heart languages of our fellow worshipers. That is the most important thing that can be said about our subject. If we remember it, we will be more sympathetic to the concerns of others and more willing to serve them rather than ourselves. Our singing, then, will express a higher quality of love for one another. And, most of all, God will be pleased.

Questions for Discussion

1. Does Scripture give us any idea why God commands the use of music in worship, rather than, say, fireworks or yoga? What would that reason be?
2. What is the purpose of music in worship? Or are there many purposes? What are some of them?
3. Have any people ever left your church, or failed to join, because they didn't like the music in your worship service? What was the issue? How would you have resolved it?
4. Why is music so important to worshipers? Why are controversies over music often more heated than other disagreements in the church?
5. Should worship be popular in style? Why or why not?
6. Discuss the recurring generation gap in the history of hymnody. What creates it? Is there one in your congregation? What can you do about it?
7. Is it wrong for hymns to reflect human subjectivity? Must hymns always be doctrinally orthodox? Should they be theologically "rich"? Should they have the highest musical and poetic quality? Why or why not?

8. What is a "musical language"? When Paul teaches in 1 Corinthians 14 that worship should be intelligible, does that teaching require attention to the church's musical language as well as its spoken language? Why or why not?

Notes

[1] I shall discuss later the justification for using musical instruments in worship.

[2] It is sometimes hard to determine in Scripture whether a particular passage was or was not originally written to be sung, especially since prose, poetry, and music are not sharply separable. However, both nonmusical poetry and song seem to me to differ from prose for roughly the same purposes. Thus, all biblical poetry is at least incipiently musical. On the continuum leading from prose to poetry, song is just a step further down the line. Therefore, it is not important for our purposes to distinguish what biblical poems were and were not originally set to music, or what specific differences of function there may be between poetry and song. Our interest is in determining how both poetry and song differ from prose. So I will speak of "poetic-musical" forms in contrast to prose.

[3] There are of course differences among biblical scholars as to what in Scripture should and should not be considered poetic. For our purposes, I am following the judgments of the NIV translators.

[4] This cannot be done, of course, apart from the work of the Holy Spirit. But the Holy Spirit works in and with the word to regenerate and sanctify. We are called to speak that word, and to speak it vividly and memorably. Thus we expect the Spirit to work through the word, whether that word is spoken or sung.

[5] This conclusion also follows from the fact that, as we saw earlier, it is not possible to draw a sharp distinction between musical and nonmusical speech.

[6] The following survey of historical church controversies is somewhat narrow. A complete account would have to consider developments in nonwhite churches, in non-Presbyterian churches, and in churches outside Europe and America. But I am trying to deal with the developments that have most heavily affected American Presbyterianism.

[7] This is true even if, as I suggested earlier, the problem results in part from the unjustified pride of younger generations. Whatever the

cause of the problem, the difference in worship language must be dealt with by loving deference on both sides. I do believe that the young should do most of the deferring; that is an implication of the fifth commandment. But the elder should not "provoke the younger to wrath."

[8]Part of the reason is simply that hymn writers in the newer style tend to be younger and less mature intellectually and spiritually. But they do grow up.

[9]Note also the Old Testament emphasis on "skillful" singing and playing of instruments (Ps. 33:3; 1 Chron. 15:22; 2 Chron. 34:12).

[10]If it were, we would have to choose the hymn or small number of hymns that we think are objectively best and sing only those again and again. Perhaps this would involve endless repetitions of pieces from the B Minor Mass! But even the best music, when overused, becomes boring.

[11]Many common criticisms of contemporary hymns are unfair, in my estimation—such as the criticism that they are too repetitious. I agree that there is room for debate on how much repetition is desirable. However, Scripture itself is often repetitious: it contains multiple narratives of the same events, multiple statements of the same doctrines, parallel thoughts in the Psalms, the repetitious "holy, holy, holy" (Isa. 6:1–3; Rev. 4:8), commands to repeat God's praises (Ps. 34:1), and repeated refrains (Ps. 136). The language of worship is more like the language of love than like that of scholarly prose. The language of love is repetitious: "I love you" has little force if it is said only once. We should renounce the intellectualism that assumes that edification occurs only in the transfer of intellectual concepts.

11

Music in Worship: Some Controversies

Exclusive Psalmody

Historically, many Presbyterian and Reformed churches have taken the position that no songs should be used in worship except versions of the Psalms. At one time, this was the dominant view among American Presbyterian churches, but it is now held only by a small minority. Nevertheless, the matter is worth discussing because of its historical importance and because it is a good test case for our understanding of how to apply the regulative principle.

The argument for exclusive psalmody is straightforward: All elements of worship must be prescribed by Scripture. Song is an element of worship. Scripture prescribes the singing of psalms. It does not prescribe the singing of any other songs in worship. Therefore, song in worship is limited to the Psalms.

I reject this argument, however, for the following reasons:

1. I argued earlier that the traditional distinction between elements and circumstances is not warranted by Scripture. Since we cannot identify elements, we cannot say that song is an ele-

ment and therefore requires specific divine commands governing its content.

2. Even if we accept the division of worship into elements, it is not plausible to argue that song is an element of worship, independent of all others. As we saw in the preceding chapter, song is not an independent element, but rather a *way* of doing other things. It is a way of praying, of teaching, of confessing, etc. Therefore, when we apply the regulative principle to matters of song, we should not ask specifically what words Scripture commands us to sing, but rather, what words Scripture commands us to use in teaching, prayer, confession, etc.

3. Even if we grant that song is an element of worship, we should note that advocates of exclusive psalmody do not treat song in the same way that they treat other elements. The type of argument used to prove exclusive psalmody could equally prove that we must use only prayers and sermons written in Scripture.[1] However, even the strongest advocates of exclusive psalmody allow both extemporaneous preaching and free prayer in worship.

4. Does Scripture command us to sing the whole book of Psalms? There are many commands in Scripture to sing psalms, to be sure (1 Chron. 16:9; Ps. 95:2; Col. 3:16; Eph. 5:19). However, the word *psalm* is a generic term for songs used in worship.[2] Biblical references to "psalms," then, do not necessarily refer to the canonical book of Psalms, any more than the reference to "judges" in Matthew 12:27 refers to the canonical book of Judges. Indeed, one can make as good a case that God commands us to sing the Mosaic Law in Psalm 119:54, 172.[3]

5. Advocates of exclusive psalmody maintain that God gave his people the book of Psalms as their definitive hymnbook for all time, much as he gave us the canon of Scripture to be our sole rule of faith and life. However, Scripture never says that the Psalter was given to us for this reason. And that idea is rather implausible, for the following reasons:

a. There were worship songs before the Psalter (e.g., Ex. 15; Num. 21:17; Deut. 32; Judg. 5) that were never incorporated into it. Since these songs have at least as strong a claim as the

Psalms to be inspired hymns suitable for public worship, it is unlikely that they ceased to be suitable once the Psalter was completed. Indeed, there is no evidence that at some point in history God forbade Israel to use those songs.

b. It was once common for scholars to describe the Psalter as "the hymnal of the second temple." But Scripture never says that that was the purpose of the Psalter, and that view has been challenged recently by some who have maintained that the Psalter was collected, not as a hymnbook, but as a book for meditation.[4] Of course, many individual psalms were evidently intended as songs for public worship, but there are some, like Psalm 1, that probably had a different purpose and origin. We can no longer simply assume that God gave us the Psalter as a hymnal—and as our only hymnal.

c. In Scripture, new acts of God call for "new songs" (Pss. 33:3; 40:3; 144:9; 149:1; Isa. 42:10; Rev. 5:9; 14:3). God delivers his people from Egypt, and they sing a new song (Ex. 15). He gives them water in the wilderness, and they sing (Num. 21:17). He renews the covenant and commits it to their memory with the song of Deuteronomy 32. Christ is conceived by the Spirit, and Mary responds with her Magnificat (Luke 1:46–55; compare 1:67–79; 2:14, 29–32). The picture is not one of a static hymnal given by God for all time; rather, it is the dynamic picture of God continually doing wonderful deeds and his people responding to them with shouts of praise. Just as God's deliverances elicit new prayers of thanksgiving and new subject matter for preaching, so they elicit new songs. In this regard, is it even remotely possible that the greatest divine deliverance of all, the redemptive work of Christ, should not evoke new songs?

6. Are the Psalms adequate for New Testament Christian worship? Certainly we cannot criticize their theology, since they are divinely inspired. And the Psalms do testify of Christ, as the New Testament shows in its use of the Psalter. But the Psalms present Christ in the "shadows" (Col. 2:17), in terms of the incomplete revelation of the Old Testament period (Heb. 1:1–3). Indeed, to limit one's praise to the Psalms is to praise God without the name of Jesus on one's lips.

But the completeness of redemption in Christ requires a whole new language of praise: about Jesus the God-man, his once-for-all finished atonement, his resurrection for our justification, and our union with him by faith as the new people of God. Doubtless there are anticipations of these doctrines in the Psalter, but Christian worship demands more than the language of anticipation. It demands the language of fulfillment and completeness, for that is what is distinctive about New Testament faith. It is precisely the accomplishment of God's mighty works that evokes praise in Scripture.

7. The exclusive psalmody position gives the impression of being very strict in its application of the regulative principle. But it would be possible to be even stricter. Someone might argue, for example, that since we are strictly limited to the inspired Psalms, we should sing the original Hebrew rather than translations (let alone free versifications!) made by uninspired persons. Where, after all, does Scripture command us to sing uninspired translations of psalms in public worship? However, those who sing psalms exclusively are not nearly as strict as that. Here, the exclusive psalmodists do what they accuse others of doing: they place practical limits on the strictness and consistency with which they apply the regulative principle.

8. Advocates of exclusive psalmody regularly insist that the burden of proof is upon those who advocate the use of uninspired[5] hymns in worship. They ask, Where does Scripture prescribe the use of uninspired hymns? I reply: Scripture tells us to sing in public worship, but it does not specify what we should sing there, except to urge conformity to God's revelation. We therefore have the liberty to make our own decisions on that matter, according to the general rules of the Word. In this respect, song is like preaching and prayer. Thus, Scripture authorizes us to sing uninspired hymns, just as it authorizes us to pray uninspired prayers and to preach uninspired sermons.

9. Similarly, someone will ask, Why do you need uninspired hymns when you have the inspired hymns of God's word, which are far superior? The answer is: for the same reasons that we must supplement the teaching of God's word with our own uninspired

of the temple ritual; it occurred many years before the temple was erected.

2. The Bible never says that all parts of the temple service were abolished by the work of Christ. The temple itself, of course, was destroyed in A.D. 70, and the distinctive worship of the temple, the offerings of food and drink, were abrogated by the finality of Jesus' atonement. The veil of the temple was torn in two when Jesus died (Matt. 27:51), indicating that he had opened the way into the presence of God. But many things done in the temple are things we still do today. The temple was not only a place of sacrifice, but also a house of prayer (1 Kings 8:28–53; Isa. 56:7; Matt. 21:13) and a place where God heard oaths and confessions of his name (1 Kings 8:31–33). It was also a center for the teaching of God's word (Luke 2:41–52). Food and drink sacrifices are not part of Christian worship, but prayers, oaths, confession, and teaching certainly are. We cannot, therefore, argue broadly that the entire worship of the temple has been abrogated. Rather, we must look at each individual aspect of temple worship to determine whether God has withdrawn his authorization for that aspect.

3. In the case of musical instruments and choirs, that is very difficult to do. In temple worship, the purpose of the instruments, even during the sacrifices, was not merely to be an accompaniment to the sacrifices, but to lead the singers in praise. Praise is something that clearly continues into the New Testament order. And, as we have seen, instruments were not limited to the temple worship. Rather, they seem to have been normal accompaniments to the praise of God's people. I know of no passage of Scripture in which singing occurs that is demonstrably unaccompanied.

4. It is sometimes pointed out that Jewish synagogues in the time of Jesus did not use instruments. It would be interesting to know why they excluded instruments, but we do not, and so we cannot assess whether they did it for a theological reason that might still be relevant to Christian worship.[6] In any case, the practice of the synagogue is not normative for Christian worship.

5. Presbyterian churches that disavow instruments usually

teaching, or the prayers of God's word with our own uninsp
prayers. Although God's word is definitive, he appoints teac
to help people to understand it. Teaching, of course, neces
ily uses words different from those in the Scriptures themsel
Hymns are a form of teaching in Colossians 3:16, and will th
require words different from those in Scripture. Also, we mu
apply the biblical language to our own situation, our own tin
and place. That means, first, applying it to the post-Resurrectio
period, and, second, applying it to the situations of the presen
day. Doing that requires us to use words that are different from
those in Scripture.

Instruments, Choirs, and Soloists

Many of the same people who restrict song in worship to the
Psalms disallow the use of instruments, choirs, and musical solos
in worship. On the surface, this second issue does not seem to
pertain to the regulative principle. There are many commands
in Scripture to use instruments in worship (e.g., Pss. 68:24–25;
98:4–6; 149:3; 150:1–6), and God ordained choirs as part of the
temple worship (1 Chron. 15:16). However, some have argued
that instruments and choirs were part of the distinctive worship
of the Old Testament temple, and that since the temple worship
has passed away in Christ, there is no warrant for the use of instruments and choirs in the church today. In the following
points, I will reply to this argument and address the related question of soloists.

  1. Instruments were indeed used in the temple worship, but
they were used on other occasions as well. For example, after
God brought Israel across the Red Sea, the people sang the song
of Exodus 15 to the Lord, to the accompaniment of Miriam's
tambourine (v. 20). Miriam sang the song to a group of women
who followed her with tambourines and dancing. Here we find
an instrument (the tambourines), a choir (the women), and a
soloist (Miriam)—not to mention dance, which we shall discuss
later. This event was unquestionably public worship: all Israel was
gathered to hear and join their praise to God. And it was not part

allow the use of pitch pipes to get the congregation started on the right note. But if a church may use an instrument to help people find the first note, why not also the second, and the third? And if the soprano notes may be assisted, why not also the alto, tenor, and bass notes? And if instruments may guide the melody and the harmony, why should they not also help the congregation maintain the proper rhythm and tempo?

6. Scripture does not require that all singing be done by the whole congregation. In fact, some psalms seem to be arranged for antiphonal or call-response performance: see Psalm 136, for example, and the alternation of curses and blessings in Deuteronomy 27:12–13 and Joshua 8:30–35. Choirs and soloists simply represent divisions in the labor of worship. It is good to sing; it is also good to meditate while others are singing.

7. Why would God permit instruments and choirs in the temple, and then forbid them in Christian worship? God does not usually issue such commands arbitrarily, without giving any reason. He does have a right to do that, but he almost never uses that right. God's commands are always edifying: they teach us about him and his ways. Some have speculated that God permitted complicated worship in the Old Testament, with instruments and choirs, because of the people's immaturity or hardness of heart, but prescribed unaccompanied song without choirs in the New Testament since that sort of music is more "simple" or "pure." But Scripture never says this. It never suggests that unaccompanied song is somehow simpler or purer than accompanied song, or even that simplicity as such is desirable in worship. Indeed, Scripture never compares the value of accompanied to unaccompanied song. The lack of any clear purpose or reason makes the exclusionist view far less plausible.

Songs Without Words

What about the playing of instruments without the singing of texts? Churches often have instrumental preludes, interludes, offertories, and postludes. Are these legitimate? I believe that these do have legitimate purposes.

1. It is proper to consider the background for worship. Worship is often distracted by traffic noise, private conversations before the service, crying children, the clattering of coins in the collection plate, and the like. There are advantages, surely, to having instrumental music during these times, especially songs that remind the worshipers of the gospel. God has not told us what the background of these events should be, and I believe we are free to use instrumental music, even without words, during those periods.

2. Beyond that, I believe that the playing of instruments itself can be an act of worship. In Psalm 150, the instruments do not merely accompany praise; in my view, they are means of praise. They are among the creatures that in verse 6 are to praise the Lord.

3. Instrumental music can be edifying, even without words. When the organist plays a hymn known to the congregation, the congregation is reminded of the words. Beyond that, as our musical literature has developed over the years, worshipers have come to associate various types of music with scriptural themes: comfort, faith, dedication, spiritual warfare, Jesus' return (trumpets!), sorrow for sin, and so on. These associations differ from culture to culture, but they are real nonetheless. Of course, the content of music tends to be more emotional than conceptual. But Scripture itself appeals to both the emotions and the mind, as we have seen. Emotional communication, emotional edification, is as important in worship as intellectual communication, for God wants his people to be transformed in every area of their lives. Therefore, songs without words can be a legitimate way of expressing God's word in worship.

Music of the Body: Dance, Lifting Hands, and Clapping

People communicate, not only by word, but also by body language. In this we image the God of Scripture, who communicates both through spoken word and through natural revelation. Some (especially Presbyterians like me) prefer to worship quietly in a sitting position, but to most people in the world it is natural to accompany words with physical actions. Recall the spiritual, " 'Sit down, servant—' 'I can't sit down! My heart's so happy that I can't sit down!' "

Hence, God's people often dance in praise, and God approves of it—see Ex. 15:20; 1 Sam. 21:11; 29:5; 2 Sam. 6:14; Pss. 30:11; 149:3; 150:4; Jer. 31:13. I have cited a large number of passages because I have actually heard people question the propriety of dance as worship on the ground of the regulative principle! Such an argument is preposterous, except on the assumption that the regulative principle exists solely to perpetuate the status quo.

It is true, of course, that God does not prescribe dance specifically for the regular worship of the synagogue,[7] tabernacle, or temple. Some have used this fact to argue that God permitted dance only on the few occasions when the Bible mentions it. But Psalm 150:4 will not let us limit dance to a few historical occasions. It is for all the people of God. I look at it this way: God is pleased when we dance before him in worship, but he does not expect us to do it every time we meet in his name. Like the activities discussed in the following paragraph, it is not a "necessary element" of worship, but something that provides enrichment of worship from time to time.

I should also mention the command to "clap your hands" (Ps. 47:1; compare Ps. 98:8; Isa. 55:12) as a response to God's salvation, and the "lifting up of hands" (Neh. 8:6; Pss. 28:2; 63:4; 134:2; 141:2; 143:6; Lam. 2:19; 3:41; 1 Tim. 2:8). This too is "music of the body." God wants body as well as spirit to be engaged in his worship. Clapping expresses joy; lifting the hands is a way of drawing toward God as the object of our worship and the source of our blessing.

Of course, there are legitimate questions about what kind of body language is appropriate for worship. In our modern culture, both popular dance and classical ballet have become saturated with eroticism, and often a perverted eroticism at that. Many churches would rather prohibit liturgical dance altogether than to allow people in sexually provocative leotards to go prancing down the aisles of the church. That concern is one which I share. However, it would not be right, because of such concerns, to dismiss entirely a form of worship that God commands.

I would suggest that in the church "sacred dance" should be first a spontaneous response to God's blessing. If people want to stand up and move rhythmically to the songs of praise, they should be encouraged to do so. Dance in worship is first of all the simple, natural, physical dimension of the reverent joy we share in Christ. Most of us, even those who are not very demonstrative in our worship, find it natural to sway, however slightly, to the rhythm of the songs we sing. That movement itself is a simple form of dance. If that is justifiable, who is to draw the line to show precisely how much movement is permitted? And if such simple movements are justifiable, why not greater movement, especially in view of the biblical references to dance?

As we consider more disciplined, elaborate, and skillful forms of dance, the church needs to engage in some prayerful thought. We should not simply accept the existing cultural dance forms, but we should seek to do something distinctive, which clearly expresses scriptural truth and emotion. In this quest, we are more likely to get help from the folk dance traditions of the world than from the highly eroticized dance forms of modern society. In any case, the meaning of dance as praise to God should not be left to the worshipers' imaginations or to the discernment of professional musicologists. Of the dances I have witnessed, those which conveyed best the joy of Jesus were dances coordinated with well-known hymn tunes on biblical themes. As the meaning of these hymns was underscored and enhanced by the dancers, I found that in watching them I became more and more a worshiper and less and less a liturgical critic.

Questions for Discussion

1. What are the best arguments for exclusive psalmody, and for excluding instruments and dance? How would you respond to those arguments?

2. What would you gain if your church decided to sing only psalms? What would you lose?
3. Have you ever been blessed by an instrumental piece in church? By a liturgical dance? Have you ever been offended by such an experience? Tell about it.
4. Would you be embarrassed to lift your hands in worship? To clap your hands? To dance? Or would it be liberating to worship with the body as well as the mind?

Notes

[1]All of the sermons in Scripture are, in the nature of the case, inspired sermons: sermons by prophets, by Jesus, and by apostles. Therefore, one could argue that there is no warrant in Scripture for "uninspired preaching." The same could be said for prayer.

[2]The terms *hymn* and *song*, which are found in Col. 3:16 and Eph. 5:19 are, as exclusive psalmodists maintain, found in the headings of the book of Psalms. However, they too are generic terms for religious songs. Stephen Pribble has analyzed this terminology thoroughly and persuasively in *The Presbyterian Advocate,* November-December, 1993, 25–30, and he reaches the conclusion advocated here.

[3]With regard to Col. 3:16, it is evident that Paul does not have Old Testament psalms in mind when he refers to the singing of the church. In this singing, it is specifically the word of Christ that dwells in us richly and in all wisdom.

[4]See, for example, J. McCann, *A Theological Introduction to the Book of Psalms* (Nashville: Abingdon, 1993); G. Wilson, *The Editing of the Hebrew Psalter* (Chico, Calif.: Scholars Press, 1985); various articles in *The Shape and Shaping of the Psalter,* ed. J. McCann, JSOT Supplement 159 (Sheffield: JSOT, 1993).

[5]The word *uninspired* in such contexts is, of course, used in the technical theological sense. An uninspired hymn is simply a hymn that is not authored by God. In this sense, the term makes no judgment on the aesthetic value of the work.

[6]We may conjecture as to the reasons. It may have been that most synagogues were too small to have trained musicians among them. Or perhaps the setting aside of the harps, as in Ps. 137:2, was symbolic of Israel's refusal to play music while under oppressive rule. Or, perhaps under the influence of Plato, the Jews feared that instruments might

improperly arouse the emotions (see Plato, *Republic,* bk. 3, a passage that may also have unduly influenced the Reformers). Certainly, we cannot assume that their decision in this matter was scripturally based.

[7]Of course, as we have seen, nothing at all is specifically prescribed for the synagogue.

12

Music in Worship: Choosing Hymns

The Words

From our previous discussion, it is evident that the words of hymns[1] should be both scriptural and understandable to the congregation. Only such words can fulfill the vertical and horizontal purposes of worship: honoring God and edifying people.

Although Scripture does not limit us to the exclusive use of psalm versions, we certainly cannot ignore the Psalter, either as a source of songs for our own worship, or as a model for new songs. I believe that most churches would benefit from a greater use of the Psalms in worship. They are God's word, after all, and they contain a great treasury of doctrine and godly emotion. In the contemporary church, we have a great need to learn to think and feel as the psalmists did as they approached God.

In the Psalms, there is a wonderful balance of reverence and joy, sadness and celebration, intellect and emotion, grace and judgment. There are no illusions: the psalmist knows that he lives in a wicked world, surrounded by enemies. Often, indeed, it seems that God's help is far off. The psalmist joyfully

135

praises God, but he does not think that a believer has to be happy all the time. He can be honest about his complaints, his sadness, and his distance from God. But he trusts God's promise; he recalls God's mighty works of salvation in the past and looks forward to the larger messianic deliverance to come. For him, one thing is important—to dwell with God in his house forever.

The psalmist also prays for judgment, for the destruction of the wicked, even the destruction of specific persons, who have set themselves against him and against God. This is not personal vengeance, but the opposite. " 'It is mine to avenge; I will repay,' says the Lord" (Rom. 12:19); therefore, the psalmist calls on God, rather than taking justice into his own hands. Nevertheless, he longs for the day when all the nations will know the salvation of God.

In the Psalms, we hear the voice of Jesus, David's greater son, for the New Testament puts the Psalms on his lips. Jesus is the great king, despised and forsaken by men, but he looks to God's word to guide his ministry and fulfills God's promises of deliverance. Jesus also speaks in the Psalms as the one who one day will judge the wicked, but who, for his people, takes God's judgment upon himself. And he sends his apostles forth to bring all nations into his everlasting kingdom.

I leave it to the reader to recognize that these themes are not always adequately reflected in modern hymns. Certainly a greater use of the Psalms will deepen our understanding of Scripture and our relation to God.

We can also learn from the Psalms about the variety of songs that may be used in worship. Some psalms are long, while others are short. Some are didactic, while others are more lyrical. Some are very simple, while others are highly complex. Some utilize elaborate literary forms such as acrostics[2] and multilevel chiasms,[3] others do not. Some are addressed to God, while others are addressed to human beings. This variety should make us less critical of hymns that we may think are too simple, too long, too short, and so on. There is room in God's worship for hymns of many kinds—for many purposes, many different kinds of people, and many learning styles.

The Psalms still have much to teach us. But, as I indicated in the last chapter, we do need hymns beyond those in the Psalter, to express the same truths in contemporary language and to apply them to our historical situation. By "our historical situation" I mean (1) the period between Jesus' resurrection and his return and (2) the distinctive nature of our own time, place, and culture.

The fact that we live after Jesus' resurrection warrants some difference from the Psalms at least in the emphasis of our worship. The truths stressed in the New Testament concerning Jesus' miraculous birth, teaching ministry, crucifixion, and resurrection are only dimly foreshadowed in the Psalms. Furthermore, many prominent teachings in the New Testament are relatively obscure in the Psalms, such as the teaching that we are justified by faith in the finished sacrifice of Christ; that we have died with Christ to sin and have been raised with him for our justification; that the Holy Spirit dwells in us as his temple, witnessing that we are children of God; that Jesus intercedes for us in heaven at God's right hand; and that he sends us throughout the earth to tell all men about him.

Our post-Resurrection position in history also makes our worship emotionally different from that of the Psalms. The longings, the laments, the questions, and the prayers for judgment in the Psalms find answers in Christ. Of course, we continue to long for the final end of sin and suffering. But the great fact of New Testament worship is the resurrection of Jesus, in which the last days have begun. We celebrate that great event (even by worshiping on a different day of the week) which the psalmists could only anticipate in the future. Surely there is rightly a greater dimension of joy in post-Resurrection worship, and a lesser emphasis on lament, complaint, and the delay of God's purposes.

Also, the element of imprecation (calling on God to judge the wicked) should be less prominent in New Testament Christian worship, though not absent altogether. It is significant that Jesus rebuked James and John for asking him whether they should call fire down from heaven upon a Samaritan village that

had not welcomed him (Luke 9:51–56). Elijah had called down
the fire of judgment (2 Kings 1:10, 12), but that was not a proper
request for Jesus' disciples. One day, wicked cities will be pun-
ished (10:8–15), but not now. This is the day of grace. Jesus came
the first time not to judge, but to save (John 3:17; 12:47). The
Christian need not be as puzzled as was the psalmist at the delay
of judgment, for the New Testament teaches us clearly that there
is to be an interval between the Resurrection and Jesus' return,
in which the gospel is offered to the world and judgment is de-
layed. That period is one of suffering for the church. Our comfort during that time is not the thought that God may destroy
our enemies tomorrow—although he may. Our comfort is that
the sufferings of this world cannot be compared with the glory
that is to follow (Rom. 8:18). It is our privilege to suffer now for
Christ's sake, so that we may be glorified with him (1 Peter 1:1–8;
4:12–19).

This is not to deny the legitimacy of imprecation today; indeed, there are imprecations in the New Testament as well as in
the Old (see Matt. 23; 26:23–24; 1 Cor. 16:22; Gal. 1:8; 5:12; 2 Tim.
4:14). It is right to call on God to judge the terrible wickedness
of our world today. But because Christ has come, we can now
pray also that the sins of these wicked people will be judged, not
individually, but in Jesus as their substitute, as God graciously
puts faith into their hearts.

We also differ from the psalmist in that we live in the modern or postmodern world. Obeying God's command to teach his
word, we seek in our hymns contemporary ways to present his
promises, his comforts, and his challenges, so that our worship
will be intelligible to the congregation and to visitors.

So, our hymnody should include the Psalms, and also
hymns that are both like and unlike the Psalms in various ways.[4]

The Tunes

We do not know the tunes that Israel used in worship during the
Old Testament period. Suzanne Haik-Vantoura has argued that
some of the markings in the Hebrew text of the Psalms are mu-

sical notations indicating melodies and rhythms.[5] But even if this is so, we do not know how old those markings are or whether they were part of the original text.

We can get some idea of the character of the ancient music by noting references in the Psalms to instruments and other aspects of song. The texts indicate a wide variety of instruments, similar to our modern harps, trumpets, flutes, percussion, and guitars.[6] To those who object to the use of guitars and drums in worship, I would comment that the instruments mentioned in the psalm headings look more like modern guitars and percussion than modern pianos and organs. I do not believe that we are limited to the instruments mentioned in Scripture, but in considering how to set hymns to music, the biblical instrumentation can give us some clues.

God's praise also included, as we have seen, dance and clapping. Some texts urge us to praise God with a loud noise or "shout" (Pss. 33:3; 98:4; 100:1), or with "resounding cymbals" (Ps. 150:5). God's approach is typically accompanied by loud noises (see Ex. 19:16; Isa. 6:4). From these data, and from the instruments mentioned above, I would conclude that the ancient music was often strongly rhythmic and loud. I would not be surprised if some of it would sound rather raucous to those accustomed to the subdued and stately music of traditional hymnody. Yet there are also psalms, and parts of psalms, which by the nature of their words seem to demand a more quiet setting, such as Psalms 23; 46:10; 131:1–3. Since, as we have seen, the Psalms are richly varied in their content and literary structure, we would expect the musical settings to be varied as well.

The chief rule for musical settings is that they reinforce, rather than detract from, the message of the words. This is not to deny the point I made in chapter 11, that music has content of its own, which can edify even apart from words. But when music and words are used together, the two should blend; they should support one another.

There are obvious rules of thumb: loud, rhythmic settings for joyful, triumphant texts; quiet, meditative settings for hymns of comfort in sorrow. We should, however avoid simplistic assumptions about what music "must" go with what texts. In modern Western society, we usually express joy in major keys, while minor keys often express sadness. But that is not the case universally. In the Near East, for example, tunes in minor keys can be joyful, fast, and rhythmic, as the Jews for Jesus have taught us in recent years.

As another example: I was recently taken aback when a church pianist played "Blessed Quietness" with a rollicking gospel 4/4 beat that got the racially mixed congregation clapping and shouting. Initially, there seemed to be a discrepancy between the words and the arrangement. But as I sang and listened, something about it seemed really right. When those billows sweep over your soul and God replaces them with his quietness, that can be an occasion for shouting. These inner-city people understood that from experience, and they sang from the heart. I had no criticism to offer.

These examples suggest that there are cultural differences in the ways that music expresses moods and thoughts. In our modern multicultural society, this is important to remember. Just as the French, German, and English languages differ in the words used to express thoughts, so Anglo, Jewish, and black cultures differ in the musical styles by which they express their faith. There are different "musical languages," just as there are different spoken languages. Indeed, as I indicated in chapter 10, even within the same culture there are different musical languages, such as the difference between the music of the old and the music of the young. What one considers joyful, the other may hear as irreverent; what one considers reverent and dignified, the other may see as joyless and dull.

Therefore, if we are to pursue the biblical goal of intelligible worship (1 Cor. 14), we should seek musical settings that speak the musical languages of our congregation and community. To do this is not to cater to human taste, but to honor God in his desire to edify people in his worship. We should not selfishly insist on using music only from our own favorite tradition. Rather, in the spirit of Christ the servant, we must be willing to sacrifice our own preferences in order to reach others with the truth. The Great Commission turns us outward, rather than inward: it calls us even in worship to reach out to those who are ignorant of Christ and of our musical traditions.

It is a good idea, then, for all of us to learn to appreciate music that doesn't immediately appeal to us. In that way we serve one another, and we also grow by learning to praise God in new ways.

Not every tune or arrangement, of course, is appropriate for worship. It is hard to draw the line precisely here. History is such that styles considered inappropriate in one time and place are taken for granted in others. One cannot specify any musical style that will definitely be appropriate or inappropriate in all times and places. But each of us must judge what is appropriate in our own cultural setting. And we know that there are some styles of music (e.g., "heavy metal" rock) that are so deeply associated with the most degenerate elements of our society that for most of us they could hardly be anything other than counterproductive to worship. Of course, hundreds of years from now some people may find in heavy metal precisely the musical language best suited to their praise. Of course, much would have to change in the cultural connotations of that music before the church should consider its use in worship.

Although we can agree to a large extent as to what is appropriate, there will also be disagreements. As I have said, we should in these cases be willing to sacrifice our personal tastes for the edification of our brothers and sisters. But what if the disagreement is more than a matter of taste? What if it is a matter of conscience, where someone is convinced in his heart that the music (or other aspects of worship) of his church is unacceptable to God?

I believe this problem should be handled in terms of Romans 14. The one who is offended should raise the issue with the church. If the church does not accept his complaint or persuade him to abandon it, then it should treat him as a believer with a "weak conscience." A "weaker" believer is one who loves the Lord, but his conscience is bound by scruples without basis in God's word. The church cannot be captive to the false scruples of weak believers. It should seek to instruct them. But if they will not be instructed, and if they cannot persuade the church to change its practice for their sake, they may have to seek other fellowships in which they can worship without violation of their conscience. Even a weak conscience, Paul says, should not be violated.

There are people who will say that they just "cannot" worship using music of one style or another. Sometimes, such complaints are legitimate. But in the typical dispute, some people argue that contemporary music sounds cheap and unworthy. (Perhaps it sounds too much like the secular music that they associate with their sinful past.) Others argue that traditional music seems dull and formal, so that it doesn't seem to amount to "real worship."[7] I believe that Scripture would classify both of these groups as "weaker" believers (Rom. 14). Paul urges believers in such disputes to stay together, loving one another in Christ, neither despising nor judging one another. But, as we know, sometimes these disputes do lead to divisions.

Such divisions are defeats, not triumphs. The goal of history is the gathering of a vast multitude from every kingdom, tongue, tribe, and nation, joining in praise to God together. The gospel breaks down the barriers between Jew and Gentile, rich and poor, bond and free, male and female. We should be expecting in our churches—particularly in our worship, when God draws near to us—surprising discoveries of unity. One way God works among us, then, is when we learn one another's music.

Questions for Discussion

1. How should our hymns be like the Psalms? How should they be different? Why?
2. In the 1970s, Idi Amin, the ruler of Uganda, slaughtered a great number of Christians because of their faith. Many Christians around the world prayed that God would depose or even destroy him. Were they right to pray that way? Why or why not?

3. Does Scripture give us any guidance about the musical tunes that we should use in worship? Discuss.

4. What "musical languages" are spoken in your community? How might your church change its style of music in order to reach those people better?

5. Do you have a preference for one particular style of church music? Do you know when that style arose and where it came from? Can you learn to appreciate other styles?

6. If you had your "druthers," what style of music would predominate in the worship services of your church?

7. How would you modify your answer to question 6 in the light of the Great Commission and the principle of edification?

Notes

[1] In this chapter I am using the term "hymns" broadly, to include all songs used in worship. That includes, therefore, psalm versions, traditional hymns, gospel choruses, Scripture songs, etc.

[2] An acrostic is a poem in which each line begins with a successive letter of the alphabet. In Ps. 119, for example, each of the first eight verses begins with the first letter of the Hebrew alphabet, *aleph;* vv. 9–16 all begins with the second letter, *beth;* and so on.

[3] In a chiasm, ideas are stated in a certain order, say, A, B, C; then the same ideas (or similar one, or ideas on the same general topics) are repeated in reverse order, C, B, A. Consider Ps. 1:

    A. God's verdict (blessing) on the righteous (v. 1).
      B. The prosperity of the righteous (vv. 2–3).
      B. The destruction of the wicked (vv. 4–5).
    A. God's verdict (curse) on the wicked (v. 6).

[4] For some thoughts about literary quality and the generation gap between traditional and contemporary styles, see chap. 10.

[5] Suzanne Haik-Vantoura, *The Music of the Bible— Revealed* (San Francisco: Bibal Press/KDH, 1990). The tunes resemble Gregorian chants.

[6] Hebrew *kinnor,* Greek *kithara,* English *guitar.*

[7] Compare our discussion in chap. 7 of "Authenticity in Worship."

13

Putting It Together

I would like to conclude this book on a practical note by indicating how I try to follow biblical principles in planning an actual worship service. I am in charge of worship as associate pastor of New Life Presbyterian Church in Escondido, California, and in that capacity I choose the hymns, determine the general order of events, play the piano, and preside from the keyboard during the singing.

When New Life Church moved to Escondido in 1980, we gave prayerful thought to the kind of worship we would have. The Escondido Christian Reformed Church was very similar to New Life doctrinally, but had a traditional Reformed style of worship and ministry. We did not want to duplicate what they were doing and, in effect, compete for the same group of potential members. Rather, we wanted to reach out to those who were not likely to visit the Christian Reformed Church: those of broadly evangelical backgrounds and those who were simply unchurched. Californians in these categories tend to be turned off by formal liturgies and by ministries that emphasize denominational traditions.

Therefore, we determined on a style of ministry that we believed was scriptural, but more intelligible (1 Cor. 14, again!) to those we wanted to reach with the gospel. We recalled Paul's intention to be as a Jew to the Jews and as a Gentile to the Gentiles, "so that by all possible means I might save some" (1 Cor. 9:22). So we determined to have a less formal worship service—but, of course, one that met the biblical criteria for true worship. Not all of us were personally thrilled by this decision. My own musical training was exclusively classical, and the thought of having to learn to play contemporary Christian music was not initially welcome to me. But Scripture kept telling us not to please ourselves, but to hear again our Lord's Great Commission.

Above all, I want you to understand that we did not make this decision in order to be up-to-date, or to entertain unbelieving visitors, or to cater to human tastes. Quite the reverse. We sought only to be faithful to the mandates of God's word, even when they ran contrary to our own preferences.

God did bless the church with substantial growth. When we moved to Escondido, about twenty-five people attended regularly. Today there are 325 communicant members.

I shall now describe the worship at New Life on a particular Sunday, February 5, 1995. Associate Pastor Bill Crawford preached a sermon on Daniel 1 called "All God's Children Need Bifocals." As he explained to me several weeks before the service, the emphasis of the sermon was on understanding the sometimes distressing events of our lives with the wisdom of Christ. Bill emphasized that Daniel and his friends, faced with the distress of being exiled to a strange land, nevertheless were faithful to God in their decision not to eat the king's food (vv. 1–16), and God honored them by giving them special wisdom (vv. 17–21). The wisdom and the faithfulness went together.

I planned the worship to reinforce the themes of the passage. After an improvised piano prelude, Elder Dave Edling welcomed the people, made some brief announcements, and then reminded the people that they were gathered to worship God. We rarely have a formal call to worship, but it was certainly evident at that point what the meeting was about.

Before worship, the atmosphere was pretty noisy, despite my

prelude. We have decided that that is what we want. We would rather have a welcoming atmosphere than a quiet time for additional prayer and meditation. There are plenty of opportunities for prayer and meditation during the service and throughout the day; there are few opportunities to meet and welcome one another and to welcome visitors to the service. In reaching our decision, the Great Commission and our love for one another in Christ were the determining factors.

After Dave's introduction, I asked the people to stand and sing a contemporary, lively praise song based partly on Psalm 98:1, 4–6. This served as a kind of corporate call to worship. Contemporary Scripture songs are sometimes criticized for containing only individual verses and snippets of Scripture passages. But almost nobody sings entire psalms without any deletion— not even exclusive Psalm singers. And I would rather have the congregation sing "snippets" that they learn very well than drag their feet through an arrangement that lasts ten minutes. The important thing in teaching, as in singing, is not how much content is covered, but how much is understood, how much is remembered, how much gets into the heart. Our people know and love this portion of Psalm 98, for they have sung it over and over again to a tune they remember. I doubt if they would have gotten as much from a version with nine stanzas and a nondescript tune. And, most importantly, their enthusiastic singing honored God.

I followed Psalm 98 with the well-known chorus "We Love You, Lord," in which we sing that we are raising our hearts to God (this was our *sursum corda*). We ask that in worship we may bring joy and pleasure to God's heart.

The words to our songs are placed on transparencies and projected on the front wall. (We get copyright permission to make these transparencies through Christian Copyright Licensing, Inc.[1]) Most worshipers don't have hymnals, but a few of them take hymnals in order to sing parts on some of the songs. Most of them sing looking up at the wall, and that creates a much fuller sound than when people are looking down into hymnbooks. The disadvantage of transparencies is that the absence of a hymnal (for most worshipers) makes it difficult for the congregation to learn new songs, especially songs with complicated tunes. I do sometimes take some time during the service to teach new songs to the people.

We encourage people to clap, whistle, tap tambourines, or otherwise to use their gifts to enhance the worship. We do not have a praise band, because we haven't the money to hire a professional group, nor do I have the time to rehearse a nonprofessional group. But in principle I would like to see more instrumentalists than just me. The more participation, the better. Anyone who can "play skillfully" (Ps. 33:3; 1 Chron. 15:22) and thereby contribute something positive to the worship, is welcome.

Then I led in prayer, including adoration of God's greatness and majesty and confession of our lost and guilty condition, acknowledging that we have forgiveness and access to God only through Christ. Anticipating the theme of the service, I asked God to open our eyes to see this world as he sees it, even in the midst of distress, and to give us the faithfulness to serve him single-mindedly. This was our invocation, but we don't call it that. I try to avoid liturgical-sounding language as much as possible.

I then asked the congregation to be seated, and I announced the theme of the sermon, which was also the theme of the period of singing that followed. That period usually lasts fifteen to twenty minutes. At the service on February 5, we began with the traditional hymn "This Is My Father's World." It's a great hymn, which we often use in reflecting on the beauties of God in nature. But it also leads us to meditate on the fact that "although the wrong is oft so strong, God is the ruler yet." It challenges us to see this world as God's sovereign domain, despite the wickedness all around us.

Then we sang "May the Mind of Christ," by Kate Wilkinson, an early twentieth-century hymn in a traditional style, which calls us to look at every aspect of life with the mind of Jesus.

We sang all the verses of these two hymns, although I do not believe that that is always necessary. (After all, one never reads the whole Bible at one sitting; we can never do more than take excerpts from God's truth.)

I do not use amens at the end of hymns. With some songs, they sound pretty odd—imagine "Wonderful Grace of Jesus" with a traditional "amen"—and it is awkward to use them with some songs and not others. I do add an amen to the concluding doxology—appending it, in effect, to the entire service.

I followed the two traditional hymns with a Scripture song by Kelly Willard based on Psalm 139:7–14, "Where Shall I Go from Your Spirit?" In that hymn, we confess that God is everywhere, inescapable, even in the depths of hell. The implicit application is that God is indeed the ruler over all the affairs of nations, even when those nations do not confess his name.

Sometimes I talk to the congregation during the singing period, emphasizing some aspect of the words of the songs. Most often, I say a bit about the theme at the beginning of that period, then proceed through three or four songs without comment. I try to avoid intruding my personality very much during this time. Some worship leaders can do a lot of talking without detracting from the worship, but I think it's best that I remain relatively in the background.

I have not felt any awkwardness at all in moving from traditional hymns to contemporary Scripture songs and choruses and back again. Our people are used to it, and they like it that way. I do get suggestions from some to have more contemporary songs, and from others to have more traditional hymns. (Similarly, some want more "short" songs, while others want to sing all the stanzas of everything.) Since I get these suggestions from both sides, I assume that my balance is pretty good for the congregation as a whole.

Sometimes I use more contemporary songs, and sometimes more traditional ones, depending on what best supports the theme. One general pattern that I have found edifying has been to sing one or two traditional hymns (taking advantage of the greater theological richness of that genre) and then follow them with a simple contemporary praise chorus, in which the people can meditate on the rich truths and give childlike adoration to the God who has done such wonderful things.

In this particular service, after we sang the song based on Psalm 139, I remarked to the people that this God who rules everywhere, in all human affairs, is the God to whom we bring our prayers, through Christ. Dave Edling then came forward and offered a fairly long prayer, mentioning specific needs of the church and its members.

Following prayer, Dave dismissed the young children (aged three to six) to our children's church (nursery is available for those under three). On the legitimacy of that, see my discussion in chapter 8. Children's churches are attractive to unchurched visitors, who usually have not trained their children to sit still for a whole hour and a half. We do not believe that we are obligated to honor all the preferences of unchurched visitors. But Scripture gives us the freedom to have a children's church. Should we not, in view of the Great Commission, use this freedom to enlarge our witness in the community? My own children have never gone to children's church. My wife teaches them to sit through the service, as she should. But I am glad that children's church is available for those we seek to reach with the love of Christ.

As the children were leaving the service, I asked the people to stand, and we sang "Be Thou My Vision," also obviously related to the theme of the sermon. The hymn was intended to prepare the hearts of the people to hear the word of God, and, incidentally, to cover the noise of the departing children.

Bill's sermon was very moving and helpful. One of my family members wrote him a special note about how it had enabled him better to stand for Christ in a difficult situation.

After the sermon, I asked the congregation to sing "Jesus Calls Us O'er the Tumult" ("... saying, 'Christian, follow me' "), a hymn to dedicate ourselves to live in this world as Jesus' disciples.

We did not have a formal recitation of a creed in this service, although we have done that when the preacher thinks it especially appropriate. We do not want such recitations to become "vain repetitions"; the creeds are too precious to be taken for granted. But please notice that our hymns have many creedal elements. In those hymns, we clearly profess our allegiance to Christ and to the doctrines of his grace.

After that hymn came the Lord's Supper. We have it once a month on Sunday morning. Like Calvin, I would prefer to have it weekly,[2] but I do not believe that Scripture requires any element of worship to be present in every service. Bill presided at the sacrament, teaching the congregation concerning its meaning and warning people not to partake if they were not trusting for their salvation in the righteousness of Christ alone. As the bread was distributed, we sang "Bread of the World in Mercy Broken," a hymn focusing upon our identification with Christ in his death, by which "our sins are dead." After the hymn, I improvised at the piano on the hymn melody until all were served and the elders returned to the front. Bill served them and invited all to partake. (We do not partake until all are served.)

Then Bill and the elders distributed the cup. We use grape juice, because we believe that the term *wine* in Scripture is broad enough to include grape juice, even though Jesus and the apostles almost certainly used fermented wine—and because we minister to some recovering alcoholics who would prefer not to drink alcohol. I and others at the church would personally prefer wine, but this is another example of how we seek to bend our own preferences in order to minister to as many as we can (1 Cor. 9:1–27).

During the distribution of the grape juice, we sang a contemporary Scripture song based on Jeremiah 17:7–8, "Blessed Is the Man That Trusteth in the Lord":

> . . . for he shall be like a tree, planted by the water,
> that extends its roots by the stream,
> and will not fear when the heat comes,
> but its leaves shall be green,
> and it will not worry in the year of drought,
> nor cease to yield fruit.

This hymn summed up the theme of the service well and also invoked the idea of God's nourishing us, which is also a theme of Daniel 1 and of the Lord's Supper.

During the offering, I accompanied our choir, directed most skillfully by Jean Clowney, in "Christ Is Made the Sure Foundation," arranged by Dale Wood. This was an entirely different kind of music from the other songs used in the service: minor key, lots of fanfare figures, open-fifth harmonies—somewhat in the tradition of English ceremonial music, but very lively and joyful. It was a powerful piece and summed up the whole service in Christ as the cornerstone of the church and of the Christian life.

At the end of the choir anthem, I went right into the doxology. The people stood and sang it, ending with a hearty amen. Bill then gave the benediction. Although we do not have a formal call to worship or salutation, we usually do have a formal benediction. In general, we try not to multiply ceremonial sentences unnecessarily, lest they become empty forms over time. But our people understand well the meaning of the benediction, and they delight in receiving God's blessing.

After that, announcements were made, followed by some socializing over coffee and then Sunday school for all ages. We find that attendance at adult classes is much higher if Sunday school follows the worship service.

Our evening service is a bit different. I don't plan it, but I do love it. At this time, Mark Futato, an associate pastor of the church and a professor at Westminster Seminary, plans the service, presides, and sometimes preaches.

Our morning attendance is around three hundred; our evening attendance is about seventy-five. This ratio is fairly typical of Presbyterian churches in southern California; unfortunately, there isn't much Sabbath observance in this area, which is so preoccupied with shopping, fun, and games.[3] At any rate, with our smaller evening congregation, we are able to have a service that is participative in some ways in which the morning service is not.

Mark brings a call to worship from a Scripture text, usually expounding it a bit. Then we sing: some selections are chosen by Mark; others are selected by members of the congregation. Sometimes the period of singing comes after the sermon, so that we can give extended praise to God for what we have learned in the word. There is also a period of prayer: in the evening service, members of the congregation bring prayer requests and then a number of them lead in prayer.

In the evening service, the congregation is somewhat more mature, chronologically and spiritually, although there are also a number of teenagers there, since their youth meeting follows the service. We sing both traditional hymns and contemporary songs, but the people tend to choose traditional hymns more often. In some ways, then, our evening service is more traditional than the morning service. It is somewhat less oriented toward visitors, mainly because we get far more visitors in the morning than in the evening.

Overall, our pattern of worship is not very unusual or creative. It is a "white bread" worship of singing, prayer, and preaching, typical of American Protestant worship in our century. It is not a high, liturgical service; we don't use a lot of responsive sentences or an order of events reenacting redemption. Nor, certainly, is it charismatic worship, although we do use some songs that originated in the charismatic tradition, and some of our members like to raise their hands during worship.

Worship like ours is often despised in the worship literature, which usually pleads either for more historical-traditional ceremonies, or for Puritan plainness, or for charismatic, Spirit-led spontaneity. I can see value in these other approaches, but I have no doubt that what we do at New Life is scriptural, and that is the most important thing. Although it is a "white bread" structure, we do give a lot of thought to what we say and sing, so that everything is full of Christ and his word.

We pay much attention to what Scripture says, and also to what Scripture doesn't say. That is the force of the regulative principle, which protects both the integrity of God's design for worship and the freedom that he gives us to apply his word in different situations.

Our congregation loves to worship the Lord. I believe that our worship honors him and edifies the people. What more can we ask? What more should we want? Doubtless we can do better—in our motivations, our attention, and our response. But we are confident that as we attend to God's word, his Spirit will lead us in the right paths.

Questions for Discussion

1. Distribute to the class a recent order of worship from your congregation. Go over each item. Are these items united by a theme? Is the service a reenactment of redemption? Is there some other rationale for the choices that were made?
2. Was anything in your worship service jarring? Distracting? Why? Did anything really lift your heart toward heaven? What? How?
3. What should the atmosphere be like before the service? Why?
4. What are the most important considerations for and against the use of transparencies? Amens after hymns? Recitation of creeds? The use of wine in communion? What are your conclusions in these areas?
5. How often would you like your church to serve communion? Why?

Notes

[1]For information, write CCLI at 6130 N.E. 78th Ct., Suite C11, Portland, OR 97218-2853.

[2]To be honest, I think that monthly communion is the worst of the common alternatives. If communion is held quarterly, then a church can emphasize heart preparation for it, and perhaps even hold a preparatory service. Communion then becomes something special, a festival. If it is held weekly, then it becomes an inseparable part of worship. Either of those alternatives accomplishes something important. But monthly communion has none of the advantages of the others, and it has the disadvantage of "Surprise! We're having communion today!" The only reason for having monthly communion is as a compromise between quarterly and weekly communion.

[3]However, the Escondido Christian Reformed Church, to its credit, does much better in this respect.

Select, Annotated Bibliography

Adams, James E. *War Songs of the Prince of Peace: Lessons from the Imprecatory Psalms.* Phillipsburg: Presbyterian and Reformed, 1991. A good biblical defense of the use of imprecatory prayers, but see my remarks in this volume on the difference in emphasis between Old and New Testaments in this regard.

Bogue, Carl. *The Scriptural Law of Worship.* Dallas: Presbyterian Heritage Publications, 1988. Pamphlet. A concise argument for a strict Puritan application of the regulative principle. Includes as an appendix William Cunningham's significant "Church Power in Relation to Worship."

Bushell, Michael. *The Songs of Zion.* Pittsburgh: Crown and Covenant Publications, 1980. This is the best recent argument for exclusive psalmody and unaccompanied song in worship. I disagree with it at many points, but it is learned, intelligent, and careful. It rejects, for example, the attempt to restrict the regulative principle to "formal" or "official" services; on that point and others I commend the author.

Carson, Donald A., ed. *Worship: Adoration and Action.* Grand Rapids: Baker, 1993. I found especially helpful the articles by David Peterson ("Worship in the New Testament"), Klaas Runia ("The Reformed Liturgy in the Dutch Tradition"), and Edmund P. Clowney ("Presbyterian Worship").

Davies, Glenn. "New Covenant Worship." Th.M. thesis, Westminster Theological Seminary, 1979. Davies maintains that the term *worship* refers, narrowly, to the ritual of the tabernacle and the temple, and, broadly, to the whole life of the believer as a living sacrifice and holy priesthood. He denies that there is any special sense in which the Christian meeting is "worship." The Christian meeting, rather, is for "edification." In the present book, I take issue with some of Davies's conclusions, but he shows well how difficult it is to draw sharp distinctions in the New Testament between worship and the rest of life.

Delling, Gerhard. *Worship in the New Testament.* Translated by Percy Scott. Philadelphia: Westminster Press, 1962. An important scholarly work.

Edgar, William. *In Spirit and in Truth: Ten Biblical Statements on Worship* (Downers Grove, Ill.: Inter-Varsity Press, 1976). A study for laymen of basic biblical principles.

Eire, Carlos M. N. *War Against the Idols.* Cambridge: Cambridge University Press, 1988. A scholarly study of the Protestant Reformers' attack on the use of images in churches. It deals also with broader concerns in the area of worship. I believe there is some truth to his argument that the Reformers were to some extent influenced by rationalism.

Engle, Paul. *Discovering the Fulness of Worship.* Philadelphia: Great Commission Publications, 1978. Another popular study of biblical principles of worship.

Frame, John. *The Doctrine of the Knowledge of God.* Phillipsburg, N.J.: Presbyterian and Reformed, 1987.

Gaffin, Richard B. *Perspectives on Pentecost.* Phillipsburg, N.J.: Presbyterian and Reformed, 1979.

Gillespie, George. *A Dispute Against the English Popish Ceremonies Obtruded on the Church of Scotland.* Reprint, Dallas: Naphtali

Press, 1993. This large volume is the most elaborate defense of the classic Puritan–Scottish Presbyterian view of the regulative principle, recently reprinted. Gillespie was an influential member of the Westminster Assembly.

Girardeau, John. *Instrumental Music in Public Worship.* 1888. Reprint, Havertown, Pa.: New Covenant Publication Society, 1983. Often referred to as a classic argument against the use of instruments in worship.

Gore, R. J. "The Pursuit of Plainness: Rethinking the Puritan Regulative Principle of Worship." Ph.D. diss., Westminster Theological Seminary, 1988.

———. Review of *Worship in the Presence of God,* edited by Frank Smith and David Lachman. *Westminster Theological Journal* 56 (Fall 1994): 443–47. Gore would like to simply drop the regulative principle from Presbyterian theology. I agree with many of his ideas and arguments, but I believe that the basic idea of the regulative principle, apart from the complicated Puritan amplifications of it, is scriptural.

Haik-Vantoura, Suzanne. *The Music of the Bible—Revealed* (San Francisco: Bibal Press/KDH, 1990). Argues that some of the markings in the Hebrew text of the Psalms are musical in nature and indicate tunes to which the Psalms were sung.

Hoekema, Anthony. *What About Tongue-Speaking?* Grand Rapids: Eerdmans, 1966.

Hurley, James. *Man and Woman in Biblical Perspective.* Grand Rapids: Zondervan, 1981.

Jordan, James. "Church Music in Chaos." In *Christianity and Civilization.* Vol. 2, *The Reconstruction of the Church,* edited by James Jordan, 241–65. Tyler, Tex.: Geneva Ministries, 1985.

———. *Liturgical Nestorianism: A Critical Review of Worship in the Presence of God.* Niceville, Fla.: Transfiguration Press, 1994. Reviews (unfavorably) the book by that title edited by Smith and Lachman.

———. *The Liturgy Trap: The Bible Versus Mere Tradition in Worship.* Niceville, Fla.: Transfiguration Press, 1994.

———. "Puritanism and Music." *Journal of Christian Reconstruction* 6 (Winter 1979-80): 111-33.

———. *Theses on Worship: Notes Toward the Reformation of Worship.* Niceville: Transfiguration Press, 1994.

———. *Through New Eyes.* Brentwood, Tenn.: Wohlgemuth and Hyatt, 1988.

———. *The Whole Burnt Sacrifice: Its Liturgy and Meaning.* Biblical Horizons Occasional Paper No. 11. March 1991.

    Jordan's work can be obtained from Biblical Horizons, P.O. Box 1096, Niceville, FL 32588-1096. I find it to be among the most interesting and stimulating material in the field. Jordan's view of the regulative principle is close to my own (see *Liturgical Nestorianism*), and he rightly rebukes the liturgical renewal movement (see *The Liturgy Trap*) for being more interested in aesthetics than in biblical principle. He also offers remarkably insightful studies in the structure of biblical symbolism in general and the symbolism of worship in particular (see especially his *Through New Eyes,* a biblical-theological treasure). He does not, however, convince me when he tries to derive from this symbolism strict rules for the order of worship, and I am not persuaded by his advocacy of "high" liturgy or by all of his aesthetic judgments. In my view, he does not take adequate account of what Scripture *doesn't* say or the importance of intelligibility in worship.

Kline, Meredith G. *By Oath Consigned.* Grand Rapids: Eerdmans, 1968.

———. *The Structure of Biblical Authority.* Grand Rapids: Eerdmans, 1972. This is the most important work on biblical authority since Warfield.

McCann, J. Clinton. *A Theological Introduction to the Book of Psalms: The Psalms as Torah.* Nashville: Abingdon, 1993. Says the Psalter was not collected to be a hymnbook, but a book for meditation. Nevertheless, he urges more use of the Psalms in worship.

Maxwell, William. *An Outline of Christian Worship.* London: Oxford University Press, 1936. A historical study, with orders of worship from many eras and sources. A good account of the development of the traditional liturgy.

Old, Hughes Oliphant. *Worship*. Richmond: John Knox, 1984. A useful historical study.

Ortlund, Anne. *Up with Worship!* Ventura, Calif.: Regal, 1978. One of the better books among those that seek to make worship more subjectively meaningful.

Poythress, Vern. "Ezra 3, Union with Christ, and Exclusive Psalmody." *Westminster Theological Journal* 37, no. 1 (Fall 1974): 74–94; 37, no 2 (Winter 1975): 218–35. Poythress's approach to the regulative principle is similar to mine; he and I have influenced one another in this area. He also develops some important implications of the fact that Christ sings with his people.

Pribble, Stephen. "The Regulative Principle and Singing in Worship." *Presbyterian Advocate,* November-December 1993, 25–30. An excellent study of the "psalm" vocabulary.

Rayburn, Robert G. *O Come, Let Us Worship: Corporate Worship in the Evangelical Church*. Grand Rapids: Baker, 1980. Has a number of good ideas, but I'm not always persuaded by his arguments.

"Report of the Committee on Song in the Public Worship of God." In *Minutes of the Fourteenth General Assembly of the Orthodox Presbyterian Church*. Philadelphia: Orthodox Presbyterian Church, 1947. Recently republished by Smith and Lachman in *Worship in the Presence of God*, pp. 179–92, 375–92. In keeping with the viewpoint of that volume, the minority report is placed in the text and the majority report is relegated to an appendix. The report deals with the question of exclusive psalmody. The majority report, denying exclusive psalmody, develops the correlation between singing and prayer, which I think is biblical and helpful: God gives us prayers in Scripture, but he permits us to pray extemporaneously; the same is true for song. The minority report, signed by John Murray and William Young, is one of the better concise arguments for exclusive psalmody. Early in the document, however, it postulates dogmatically that song is an "element" of worship, and if you deny that premise, the whole argument collapses.

"Report of the Committee on the Involvement of Unordained Persons in the Regular Worship Services of the Church." In *Minutes of the Fifty-eighth General Assembly of the Orthodox Presbyterian Church,* 264–79. Horsham, Pa.: Orthodox Presbyterian Church, 1991. There are majority and minority reports on the question. I find the majority report persuasive.

Ridderbos, Herman N. *Paul.* Grand Rapids: Eerdmans, 1975. A comprehensive and profound work on Paul's theology.

Smith, Frank, and David Lachman, eds. *Worship in the Presence of God.* Greenville, S.C.: Greenville Presbyterian Theological Seminary Press, 1992. This volume defends the traditional Puritan version of the regulative principle, including exclusive psalmody. There are some important essays in it, but on the whole the content is disappointing, even granting the writers' point of view. For the most part, they seem to have little understanding of why serious Reformed people have rejected the traditional position, so they don't grapple with any difficult issues; they simply reiterate the same arguments used by the early divines. In that respect, Bushell's book is far superior.

Webber, Robert E. *Worship Is a Verb* (Waco, Tex.: Word, 1987).

———. *Worship Old and New.* Grand Rapids: Zondervan, 1982. Webber is one of the leading voices urging evangelicals to adopt more of the historic liturgies.

Scripture Index

161